"**Mother Loyola's name** is becoming one that in itself is an endorsement of every book over which it appears...A careful use of Mother Loyola's work will be productive of the best results."  --Rosary Magazine, November 1901

About Mother Mary Loyola:

Most Catholics today who have heard the name Mother Mary Loyola know her as the author of *The King of the Golden City*, which has enjoyed a resurgence in popularity in recent years. But few know that she wrote over two dozen works, and that she was once a household name among Catholics of her era. What made her unique among Catholic authors was her ability to draw in her listeners with story after story—and not just any stories, but ones that incorporated current events and brand new inventions of the time. Despite the fact that those events are no longer current, and those inventions no longer brand new, her books scintillate with the appeal of an active mind that could find a moral in the most unusual places. And while the printed word lacks the animated facial expressions and vocal inflections which reveal a gifted storyteller, hers convey her enthusiasm so capably that the reader can easily imagine sitting at the feet of this wise old nun.

About *Forgive us our Trespasses*:

Mother Loyola's work on the subject of Confession is not merely groundbreaking, but seems to form one of the most crucial of her strengths, given that the Sacrament of Penance has always been the most avoidable *and avoided* of all; most Catholics express a distaste for it akin to torment. For her readers, however, such angst is inconceivable, as she does not merely help to remove all fear and discomfort associated with the Confessional; she also enkindles a deep sense of appreciation for the *gift* of the sacrament. This, in turn, fosters an eager anticipation of the grace it confers. Those who make use of *Forgive us our Trespasses*—whether children or adults— will find themselves seeking this healing Sacrament with regularity.

To learn more about Mother Mary Loyola, visit our website at
www.staugustineacademypress.com.

FORGIVE US OUR TRESPASSES

# Forgive Us Our Trespasses

◆ *Talks Before Confession* ◆

By

Mother Mary Loyola

Edited By

Reverend Herbert Thurston, S.J.

Revised and Updated By
Lisa Bergman

2011
St. Augustine Academy Press
Lisle, Illinois

This book is newly typeset based on the 1901 edition published by the Catholic Truth Society. All editing strictly limited to the correction of errors in the original text, the addition of selected footnotes, and minor clarifications in punctuation or phrasing. Any remaining oddities of spelling or phrasing are as found in the original.

**Nihil Obstat:**
SYDNEY F. SMITH, S.J.,
CENSOR DEPUTATUS.

**Imprimatur:**
HERBERTUS CARD. VAUGHAN.
ARCHIEP. WESTMON.

This book was originally published in 1901 by the Catholic Truth Society.
This edition ©2011 by St. Augustine Academy Press
All editing by Lisa Bergman

ISBN: 978-1-936639-06-9
Library of Congress Control Number: 2011941814

Unless otherwise noted, all illustrations in this book, including the cover, are either the original illustrations as found in the book, or are public domain images.
*Illustration on rear cover:*
Holy Card Heaven. http://holycardheaven.blogspot.com, June 23, 2010.

TO THE

### Sinless Virgin Mother,

MINDFUL TO SPEAK GOOD THINGS FOR US

IN THE SIGHT OF GOD,

AND TO TURN AWAY HIS ANGER

FROM US.

# Contents

| | | |
|---|---|---|
| Editor's Note | | xi |
| Preface | | xiii |
| To Young Teachers | | xv |
| I | The Devil's Traps | 1 |
| II | Two Sacraments of the Supper Room | 8 |
| III | Preparation for Confession | 17 |
| | (1) Prayer for Help | 18 |
| | (2) A Form of Examination of Conscience | 21 |
| |     Another Form of  "    "    " | 24 |
| | (3) Motives for sorrow | 26 |
| |     The effects of sin | 30 |
| |     God's hatred of sin | 31 |
| |     Hell | 34 |
| |     Purgatory | 40 |
| |     Our Heavenly Home | 45 |
| |     The Sacred Passion | 48 |
| |     The Scourging | 49 |
| |     The Crowning with Thorns | 51 |
| |     Calvary | 55 |
| |     God infinitely good in Himself | 58 |
| |   How to perfect our Contrition | 60 |
| | (4) Resolution of Amendment | 62 |
| IV | Confession | 66 |
| V | Starting Afresh | 74 |

Stories to read whilst I am waiting my turn
    The Pool of Bethsaida     85
    The Ten Lepers     87
    The Prodigal Son     89
    St. Mary Magdalen     94
    The Good Thief     97

Updated form for Confession     102

## Editor's Note

I have endeavored in this new revised edition of Mother Mary Loyola's *Forgive us our Trespasses* to be as faithful as possible to the original text as printed in the 1901 edition by the Catholic Truth Society. However, I have, in a few cases, judiciously corrected punctuation and spelling where the change significantly enhanced the clarity of the passage. I have also augmented the text with additional footnotes, in the hopes of shedding some light on personages and events which were well-known to readers at the time, but are no longer so. Therefore the reader should understand that though this text is considered revised due to these facts, the majority of the material found herein is exactly as it was written over a century ago.

In order to make this book as useful as possible for modern Catholics, one change was necessary: an update of the form for Confession. At the time this book was written, the average Catholic was familiar with the *Confiteor,* the prayer of confession used in the Mass. Today, few are familiar with this prayer, and it has been replaced in the confessional by the Act of Contrition. However, rather than replacing the original text, I have simply added an updated form for Confession as an appendix at the end of the book. In this way, it is easy to access for use in the Confessional.

Lastly, I would point out that all Scriptural references found in this book are from the Catholic Douay-Rheims version, and thus they often do not align in chapter and verse with modern bibles, which conform more closely to the chapter and verse structure of the Protestant King James Version.

In Christ,<br>
Lisa Bergman<br>
St. Augustine Academy Press<br>
May 2011

# Preface

IF it is important that in the matter of Confession children should begin well, it is not of less importance that they should be taught to take all pains in continuing the work well begun. In a First Confession much of the effort and much of the responsibility falls upon the teacher, and it is as a help to the teacher that the little book bearing that name will be most cordially welcomed. The present volume is intended much more directly for the child's own use. Its motto we might say is Self-Help. Busy as our clergy are in thickly populated districts, it is often next to impossible that the younger members of their flocks, except for an occasional word in the confessional, can meet with anything like individual interest and direction. The very pains which a parish priest takes to do his utmost for those whom he is preparing for their First Confession or First Communion prevents him from devoting much time to the children who are in an intermediate stage or who have left their First Communion behind them. These last have necessarily to depend upon their own efforts, and it is Mother Loyola's aim in the present volume to direct those efforts into right channels. The help she has offered seems eminently practical. The pitfalls against which she cautions her young readers with skilfully disguised iteration, the large choice of motives of contrition, the varied and metrical form in which she has presented these motives, thus strengthening that part of the fabric which is at once the most important and the most apt to be worn threadbare, or again, the Gospel stories provided to be read during the time of waiting outside the Confessional, all give the impression of work that has grown out of practical experience. I can only hope that the fruit produced by this little book in the souls of the young may bear some proportion to the labour and care which have been ungrudgingly spent upon it.

In order to avoid confusion with other writings of the same author, it has seemed desirable to call this little volume by a distinctive title: *Forgive us our Trespasses*. Although this may perhaps be thought somewhat fanciful, it will not, it is hoped, disguise the close connection between the present booklet and its predecessor, *First Confession*. As in the case of this last a penny book of prayers, largely taken from the pages which follow, will be issued by the Catholic Truth Society in a separate form. It may also be well to mention that a few sentences in the last chapter have been borrowed from the author's earlier work, *First Communion*.

HERBERT THURSTON, S.J.
July 31st, 1901.

# To Young Teachers

WE hear of children utterly neglecting the sacraments as soon as they are freed from control, or never presenting themselves after the first reception. There are many causes, doubtless, for this sad state of things. But what, in this country at least, may be held mainly responsible for the fact, is not so much the influence of the indifference or irreligion of those about them, as the unwillingness of the young to face what they consider an irksome duty.

It is impossible to deny that regular frequentation of the sacraments involves sacrifice. But let us beware of representing the Sacrament of Penance in any other light than that in which the Church represents it—as the Sacrament of Mercy, in which the requirements, no less than the ends, are *merciful.*

It would seem to be the devil's policy to haunt with fears preparation for confession all along the spiritual course. In its first confession the child fears the priest—that he will "scold," or "tell." Then come fears about the dispositions necessary, or about past confessions, or on the other hand, the fear generated by pure idleness that dreads the labour preparation involves. We cannot perhaps hope to prevent these disturbing fears altogether. But if anything will remove the cause, it will be a sufficiency of the Church's doctrine clearly apprehended from the first. This will also be the best foundation for the dispositions the sacrament requires.

If of any evil, then surely of scrupulosity we may say that prevention is better than cure. Better—a thousand times better—and easier is it to guide the judgment aright from the first, whilst the mind is unswayed by fear, than to attempt to rectify it once it has lost its balance. Children are not wilfully scrupulous. The evil in their case comes generally of a religious and sensitive temperament at the mercy of a conscience imperfectly instructed, and therefore open to fears which no teaching later will remove. Were they, whilst the conscience is forming, to grasp firmly a sufficiency of doctrine respecting sin, temptation, the dispositions required for approaching the sacraments, etc., would not much trouble of mind in later life be avoided?

We have not done enough for our children when we have taught them how to examine their conscience, and make an act of contrition. If the sacraments are to sustain their spiritual life up to the end, it will not suffice for the doctrine concerning them to have laid hold of the memory. It must fasten on the imagination, and sink down into mind and heart. Thus only will there be any guarantee for the future. When there is a strong conviction of the helpfulness and happiness stored up in the sacraments, when experience no less than faith recognizes them as founts of grace, regular recourse to them will not be a mere matter of duty. The children will run to them instinctively for healing and for strength, and thus ensure their perseverance in the service of God.

We spare no pains in our instructions when children are approaching the Holy Eucharist. Those who ought to know tell us that instruction on the Sacrament of Penance should be at least as careful. "It is not their Communions but their confessions we ought to trouble ourselves about," said a priest of much experience; "the Communions will be all right if we can secure the confessions."

So many excellent explanatory catechisms are in use amongst us, that anything further on the Sacrament of Penance might seem uncalled for. The excuse for this little book must be a desire to help our sorely-taxed teachers in a somewhat different direction—in drawing the hearts of children to Him Who shows Himself to us in this sacrament as the Good Samaritan, the Good Shepherd, the tender Physician of our souls, and Who chose for the institution of this Sacrament of Mercy the brightest day the world has ever seen, the day of His Resurrection from the dead.

# I
# The Devil's Traps

The food and the exercise that were good for us as little children are not enough for us later. We need something different in kind and in degree. So it is with our soul. As its powers strengthen, it must have stronger food—more useful and interesting things to occupy it—and it must put out its strength to grasp these things by trying to understand them, that it may grow up like the body, sound and strong, fit for the work God has ready for it in this world.

We have learned enough about the Sacrament of Penance to make our first confession. But there is much more to learn if the sacrament is to be to us all our life long what our Lord means it to be—our greatest help and comfort next to His own real Presence in the Holy Eucharist.

There are children in these days who give up going to confession as soon as they leave school and are able to do as they like. They give it up, and for long years, perhaps all their life, never confess the sins that get crowded together in their conscience, to be brought out every one of them when they appear before our Lord for judgment. Their last illness comes. They are told there is no hope, they must die. Then the thought of their sins rushes upon them. But they are very weak and in pain. Examination of conscience seems impossible. They cannot bring themselves to do now what they would not take the trouble to do when they were strong and well. And the devil whispers it is no use, it is too late. And so they die as they lived, without that comforting sacrament which makes us live happily in God's friendship, and die in peace with Him. They die as they lived, and with all their sins upon them appear in the presence of God for judgment.

Now why is it that some children give up the sacraments like this? I say the sacraments, for of course, if confession goes, Communion goes too. Penance is to the Holy Eucharist what St. John Baptist was to our Lord, a Precursor, going before to make hearts ready for Him. Why is it that children leave off going to confession? Because they let themselves be caught in the devil's snares. He knows that the Sacrament of Penance is God's way of saving us. It is like the bright rocket sent out from the shore, carrying with it a rope to the poor shipwrecked people struggling in the waves. If they catch hold of the rope it will draw them safe to land. The devil wants us to perish, therefore he hates confession. He hates it because he knows that all the trouble he took to get us to commit sin is of no use if we are sorry for our sins and confess them. Hence he tries to fill our minds with all sorts of silly fears about the Sacrament of Penance that he may get us to keep away from it, first for a long time, and then altogether. Let us examine his traps, and then when we know all about them we shall surely not be so foolish as to let ourselves be caught.

Traps have to be kept out of sight. The spider spins his web in dusky corners; the pit dug for the tiger is covered with branches and jungle grass. The devil's traps, too, have to be hidden. All round the confessional they are set—different kinds for different people—but all must be well concealed. That the priest will "scold" or "tell"—this is the trap for the very little children. He could not catch the bigger ones in that, for we know that out of the confessional the priest cannot, without our leave, speak even to ourselves about the sins we have confessed. If we have told him something dreadful, he cannot afterwards show by so much as a look that he knows anything about it. It is just as if he had never heard of it. We know that the great St. John Nepomucene suffered martyrdom rather than tell what he knew in confession, and that God showed the preciousness of that death in His sight by the light that shone round the holy body as it floated on the water, and by the incorruption, many years after death, of one small portion of it—*the tongue,* which had held the secret of the confessional safe.

So it is only very little children that our cowardly enemy can hope to catch in this trap. Now what has he for those who are older?

First there is the fear of trouble. It is such a bother to have to think of our sins. How can any one remember all he has done for a week or a month? How indeed! But who asks you to do this? All you have to remember are the bigger sins, for you are not strictly obliged to confess any but those that are mortal. Please God, you will not usually have mortal sins to confess, and then you must tell some of your venial sins, that your examination of conscience—which, of course, you make every night—will help you to remember. But let us stop for a moment to refresh our memory as to mortal and venial sin.

*Mortal* means deadly. Three things are required to make a mortal sin: (1) grave matter; (2) full knowledge; (3) full consent.

(1) Grave matter—the sin must be a grievous sin, that is, the thought, word, action, or omission, must be something of very great importance, *e.g.,* going to Communion after breaking

the fast; stealing a large sum, or a small sum from a person extremely poor.

(2) Full knowledge—not done by mistake or before we knew clearly what we were about. The mind must think of the act and of its sinfulness at the time the act is done.

(3) Full consent—the will must deliberately agree to the temptation, whether of thought, word, or deed.

If there was not full knowledge, or full consent, but hesitation in rejecting the temptation, or only half consent, the sin is venial, not mortal, the soul is injured but not killed.

*Venial* means pardonable. This sin is so called because it is more easily pardoned than mortal sin. A lie of excuse, a small injury to our neighbour, do not turn the soul away from God like mortal sin, and therefore do not take away sanctifying grace. Nevertheless venial sin is a great evil and should be repented of sincerely. It dis-pleases God, deprives the soul of many graces, weakens it by taking away its fear of offending God, and in this way often leads to mortal sin. No one ever comes to mortal, except through carelessness about venial sin. Each venial sin deserves its own temporal punishment and will prolong our purgatory.

The law of God is that every mortal sin is to be confessed and absolved once. But it would not be safe to confess those sins only which we know for certain were mortal. We are so apt to deceive ourselves, that it is by no means easy to form a true judgment of our past acts. We cannot know always whether there was full know-ledge and consent. Fear, shame, the wish that we had not such a sin to confess, the desire to stand well in the opinion of our confessor—these things may easily mislead us. The only safe practice is to confess whatever is on our conscience and gives us trouble—certain things as certain, doubtful things as doubtful. Those who keep things back, who have secrets about their sins, or try to settle their doubts themselves, are very unhappy. They find confession a torture, they lose their peace and their confidence in God, and perhaps give up His service altogether.

As to venial sins, they have been called to mind at our night prayers, and a very few minutes' quiet thought will bring before us two or three of the chief. For a month's confession, eight or ten minutes is abundance of time to give to examination of conscience. If you go oftener than this, less time will suffice. Is the trouble here anything to be frightened at? Will you be caught in this trap?

Here is another:

"I don't feel any happier after confession," some-body says. "I am always afraid I haven't made a good one, so I am miserable when I am getting ready, and miserable when I come away."

A sad pity, yet your own doing entirely. Your own, that is to say, and some one else's whose business it is to make confession a misery for all who will let him. But let us look a little closer into trap No. 2. You fear that you will not make a good confession. Why should you have such a fear? Two things only can make your confession bad—*wilfully leaving out a mortal sin;* or confessing it *knowing you have no sorrow for it, or purpose of avoiding it in future.* But you have only to ask for sorrow and make use of considerations that will move you to it; and to be determined to avoid all mortal sins, and the immediate occasions which lead you to commit them.

Suppose a person *had* made a bad confession, by wilfully hiding a mortal sin, or by going knowing he had no sorrow or resolve to give up that sin, he would have to set this right in a good confession in which the mortal sin was told and the hiding told, and in which there was true sorrow and purpose of amendment. This confession must go back to the last good confession, and any mortal sin committed since that time must be confessed.

But some one may say: "Perhaps there have been mortal sins that I ought to have found out in my examination of conscience, or that I have never confessed properly, and now I have forgotten them."

Supposing this to be the case, those sins were forgiven in the first good confession you made afterwards, or even before that, for hidden sins may be taken away in several ways, by an act of perfect contrition or perfect love of God, or by a good Communion. If such a sin were to come to mind later, and you were quite certain you had never confessed it, you would have to do so in your next confession, because of God's law that every mortal sin must be confessed once. But it was forgiven before you confessed it.

"But suppose I had confessed them without proper sorrow?"

If you knew at the time you had no sorrow and did not want to have it—not a likely thing you know—you would set this right afterwards in a good confession. Supposing you had no true sorrow, but thought you had, your confession would be—not bad, because you did not mean to go without contrition—but invalid, that is, there would be no sacrament, because part of the matter was wanting. The matter of the Sacrament of Penance consists of the acts of the penitent—confession, contrition, satisfaction. And as baptism with something that looked like water, but was not water, would be no baptism at all, so with confession without true sorrow. What then becomes of the sins confessed? They were forgiven in the next confession in which there was true sorrow, as forgotten mortal sins are forgiven; because in every good confession we make, we implicitly, that is, really though not expressly, withdraw our will from every mortal sin of which we have been guilty.

Where, then, is there any room for trouble about my confessions, above all if I go often and take care to do my easy part by way of preparation? What is it I am afraid of? That I may get too much grace? That my soul may become too pure, too beautiful in His sight Who has washed it so often in His Precious Blood? That my temptations may be made too light, and the trials of my life all too easy by the grace that like a full, bright river will bear me on to my Heavenly Home? Or that our Lord Who has forgiven me so often in this dear sacrament will have nothing left for judgment? For it is the same Judge in both places—in the confessional now, on the judgment-seat presently. He tries every sin once, but the place of our trial we may choose. It may be in the tribunal of mercy, where we are certain of mercy and forgiveness, both being solemnly promised to us by the Judge Himself if we but tell Him our sins with sorrow. Or it may be at the bar of His justice after death, when the time for mercy is past, and He is obliged to pass sentence according to our deserts.

The sentence once passed in either of these tribunals is never changed. What He forgives now, He will forgive always. When I fall down at His feet the first moment after death, and He asks me about my life, I shall say to Him quite simply what I have said to Him so often: "Since my last confession I accuse myself of—" Behind that last confession He will not go. Oh how happy I shall be then, if by regular and good confessions all my life, I have got forgiveness of all my sins, so that there are only good works to be presented at Judgment, and all our Lord has to do is to open His arms and say to me: "Come!"

# II
# Two Sacraments of the Supper Room

When we are going to tell others anything very wonderful, we prepare them for it beforehand, lest they should be startled and turn away saying that our words are too strange to true. Our Lord meant to give to His apostles many marvellous powers. Of these, two were so amazing that He prepared their minds beforehand, and worked two miracles to prove that His words conferring these powers were not too strange to be true. He was going to give them power to change bread into His Body and wine into His Blood. And He was going to give them the power to forgive sin.

In the supper-room on Thursday, the day before He died, He instituted the Blessed Sacrament, that is, He changed the bread He held in His Hands into His own Body, and the wine in the chalice into His own Blood.

And He gave the apostles sitting there at table with Him power to do this wondrous act. "Do this," He said, "for a commemoration of Me." These words would surely have startled them had they not been prepared beforehand. Let us see how our Lord prepared them.

One day when a hungry crowd of five thousand men and an immense number of women and children were gathered round Him in a desert place, and were hungry and had nothing to eat, He made them all sit down on the green grass. Then taking in His holy hands five loaves brought to Him by a little boy in the crowd, He lifted up his eyes to Heaven, and blessed, and broke the loaves, and gave them to the apostles to divide among the people. Five loaves among five thousand! Yet there was enough, and more than enough. Twelve baskets of fragments were taken up when they had all finished. The people saw what a miracle Jesus had done and they said, He must be the Redeemer Who was to come into the world.

The next day when they were still talking of the miracle, our Lord told them of another bread more wonderful still which He would give them some day. It would be bread from heaven. It would be enough for the whole world. It would be living bread. It would be His own true Body. Many of the Jews standing round Him began to murmur when they heard this. "How can this man give us His flesh to eat?" they said. And going away they left Him, and were not seen among His disciples any more. But the apostles did not murmur. They had seen the miracle their Master had done the day before in the desert. That miracle proved Him to be God. And so when He turned to them and said sweetly: "Will you also go away?" Peter, in the name of the rest, answered loyally, "Lord, to whom shall we go? Thou hast the words of eternal life."

A year after this Jesus was seated at supper with the Eleven. It was the last night of His life on earth, the night in which He was going to leave us His best bequest—His own real Self in the Blessed Sacrament. And the hour was come in which He was to make us this unspeakable gift. He took the bread that lay before Him on the table. He lifted His eyes to Heaven. He blessed and broke, and gave to them saying: *"This is My Body, which is given for you. Do this for a commemoration of Me. And having taken the chalice, giving thanks He gave to them saying: Drink ye all of this. This is My Blood which shall be shed for you."* Think with what trembling reverence the apostles received from those sacred hands the very Body which was to be given for them on the Cross, the very Blood which on the morrow was to be shed for them. Think with what awe they heard the words of those Divine lips, enabling them as priests to do what He had done, and to pass on their power to those who were to come after them, the priests of the one Church.

This was the first of two great powers given by our Lord to the apostles. You see how it was prefigured, or shown before, by something that was like it, and how our Lord worked the wonder in the desert, which they could see, on purpose to prove that He was God, and that they must believe Him when He should work another wonder which they could not see.

Let us look now at the second great power given by our Lord to His apostles, and notice how He prepared them in the same kind of way.

On the night of His Resurrection they were gathered together again in the Supper-room. They were talking over all that had happened during the day, and were filled—now with joy because the holy women and Peter himself had seen the Lord, and told them He was truly risen, now with fear, lest the news should be too good to be true. Suddenly, Jesus in all His risen beauty stood in the midst of them. He looked lovingly around, and stretching out His hands with the eagerness of a joygiver, said: *"Peace be to you. The disciples therefore were glad when they saw the Lord. He said to them again: Peace be to you. As the Father hath sent Me, I also send you. When He had said this, He breathed on them and said: "Receive the Holy Ghost. Whose sins you shall forgive they are forgiven them, and whose sins you shall retain they are retained."* (St. John 20.)

Did these wonderful words seem too good to be true? Did their Master really mean that He gave to them, the Eleven, power to forgive the sins of men? Yes, and they took this power from His sacred lips as three days before they had taken the power to consecrate the bread and wine. They were not startled. He had prepared them for this long before by a miracle which proved that He had Himself the power He was giving to them.

Our Lord was one day teaching in a house at Capharnaum, that city which, because of the many miracles He had worked in it, was called "His own city." He was well known there, and on this day so many had come to hear Him, that there was no room, "no, not even at the door." And still the people pressed forward, all eager to catch a glimpse of His face and hear a word from His lips. In the midst of His discourse a noise at the door caused some disturbance, and our Lord had to stop. Some men were trying to force a way into the crowded room, and His listeners turned angrily upon them. Could they not see the place was full? Whatever their business might be, the Master must not be disturbed—let them come another time. Sensible advice that seemed to produce the desired effect. All was quiet again, and our Lord continued His instruction. But presently a sound of feet and of voices overhead made His hearers look up. There was the thud of something heavy being dragged along. Then a noise as if the roof was being opened. The people wondered what was coming. Jesus sat there quietly, His eyes cast down, a smile on His lips. He knew well what was coming—who was coming, and He waited.

The roofs of Eastern houses are flat, and reached by a stairway from the yard or street. They are made of beams overlaid with dry clay or slabs of stone or tile, and are opened without much difficulty when occasion requires. But what a time was this for carrying on noisy work up there! A slab of stone was removed, and a flood of sunshine poured into the room, the bright sunshine of that sunny land. Then all was dark again. Something big had been thrust over the hole and was being let down by ropes tied to the corners. It was a mattress, and on it lay a poor man sick of a disease called the palsy. All power was gone from his weak and trembling limbs. He could not walk, or stand, or even move himself on his bed. The crowd had to move when they saw the heavy weight coming down on their heads, and presently the bed with its helpless burden lay at the feet of Jesus. The sick man was pale and trembling. It had been a difficult task to hoist him up from the street to the roof. But such was his faith and that of his friends, that danger and difficulty were counted for nothing so he might be brought to where the Master sat. The hope in his heart had made him bold. But now he was afraid with another fear, and he turned his eyes timidly to our Lord as if to ask if he had done wrong in causing all this disturbance. But one look into the beautiful Face that bent over him calmed his fears, and tears of joyful expectation ran down his cheeks, as he lifted his thin hands to Jesus.

For an instant only. Then hands and eyes dropped before the majesty of Him Who sat there. It was as if his whole life with all its sinfulness lay bare before a Judge; and thought for the poor suffering body was swept away before another desire—that *his soul* might be cured by Him Who read it through and through. Sorrow such as he had never felt before was being poured into his heart, and when again he lifted his eyes to the Face of Jesus, the tears that filled them were tears of true contrition.

Meanwhile there was silence all around. Capharnaum was used to miracles. Yet who could get used to the wondrous works of those healing hands! The blind saw, the lame walked, the lepers were cleansed, the deaf heard, the dead rose again.

There was no getting used to this. So there was a hush and breathless expectation, and our Lord's enemies, the Scribes and Pharisees, bit their lips with rage and envy as they saw the admiration with which the people looked upon the Wonderworker Who had come among them.

There was silence for a moment—and then our Lord spoke. It was not to heal the body. He had a higher and more needful work to do first. Bending over the sick man He said to him with grave tenderness: "Be of good heart, son, *thy sins are forgiven thee.*" The lookers-on were startled. They expected a cure on the body, but here was something more extraordinary still—a man claiming power over the *soul*. It was very strange; "but never did man speak like this Man;" they listened reverently and in silence.

Not all, however. The Scribes and Pharisees were filled with anger and indignation. "Who can forgive sins but God only?" they thought. They said nothing, but our Lord knew the thoughts of their hearts. Raising His head, He looked straight at them with that fearless gaze of His and said: "Why do you think evil in your hearts? Which is easier to say, Thy sins are forgiven thee, or to say, Arise and walk? But *that you may know that the Son of Man hath power on earth to forgive sins—*Arise!" He said to the sick man, "take up thy bed and go into thy house." Instantly the man arose, strong, hale, vigour in every limb. Taking up the mattress-bed, he threw it over his shoulder, and, as a cry of praise rose up all around, made his way through the throng to the door, and passing into the wondering crowd without, went to his house glorifying God.

Now notice this about the miracle wrought that day. The people did not believe our Lord to be God. They took Him to be a prophet of God, having power to heal the body, not of himself but by God's power given to him. The Scribes and

Pharisees knew He had this power, because they had proofs of it in the cures He did every day. But they would not believe God had given Him, a man, the power to heal the soul. What did our Lord do? Did He say to them, "You are right, God only can forgive sin. But I am God, and by My Divine power I forgive this poor man his sins?" Did He say this? No. He took away the disease of the body by a cure they could see, *to prove that God can give to man power to take away the disease of the soul* by a cure they could not see. *"That you may know the Son of Man hath power on earth to forgive sin,"*—this, He says expressly, was what moved Him to heal the body of the paralytic on that day.

No wonder He stopped His preaching; and sat so patiently whilst the roof was broken in. He had come to the house, not to delight a crowd of attentive listeners, but to be stopped by the disturbance, and have the sick man laid at His feet, and through a cure worked before their eyes, to prove to those gathered together there, that God *can* give to man His own power of forgiving sin. The simple people who, unlike the Scribes and Pharisees, were not hindered by pride and envy from believing, took the proof that was given them "and glorified God that gave such power to men."

"To men." You see the people believed, and rightly, that this power was given to one who was a man, to Jesus of Nazareth. Now was it ever given to others? Did Jesus Christ our Lord, Son of Man, give to men the power of forgiving sins in His name? We have seen already. On the night of His Resurrection from the dead He stood among His apostles once more. He came to tell them that, weak and cowardly as they had shown themselves during the time of His Passion and death, He had forgiven all, and was going to make them His helpers in the work for which he had come into the world. This work was to save us from sin and hell and to teach us the way to heaven.

He had saved men by dying for them. They were to save men by applying to each soul the forgiveness of sin which His death had bought for it. *"As My father hath sent Me"* He said, *"I also send you...Whose sins you shall forgive they are forgiven."*

Of what use would all our Lord has done for us have been, had He not left upon the earth a power to deal with sin? Without it, even the gift of Himself in Holy Communion would have been in vain. For how many guests would there be for the Feast He has prepared, had He left no means of getting back that wedding-garment without which no one may sit down at His table?

What He thinks of this precious fruit of His Passion, we may see by His haste in bringing it to us as soon as it was won, the very day He came back to us from the grave. He would not institute this sacrament together with the Eucharist on Maundy Thursday. He waited for Easter Day, the gladdest of all days, when every thought, and word, and act of His was glad. And truly it was fitting that the sacrament which has raised so many millions of her children from death to life, should be given to the Church on the Feast of life, the Feast of His own Resurrection. Others were instituted later, during the forty days He remained on earth. But the sacrament of reconciliation and peace stands quite alone on Easter Sunday, the joyful evening gift of that day of joy.

What did the apostles think of this gift? They had not room for much in their creed, but there must be room for the "forgiveness of sins." And see in what charming company they put it—"the communion of saints, the resurrection of the body, and life everlasting." Let us think of this gift and thank Him for it joyfully when we come to these words in the creed.

Of course our Lord never meant the power given to the apostles to stop when they died. It would be needed by every man, woman, and child to the end of the world. It would be needed by you and by me just as much as it was needed when the apostles were on earth. "I am with you all days even to the end of the world," our Lord said to them. And He told them that penance and remission of sins should be preached in His name unto all nations. This could not be done by the Apostles themselves, who were not to live to the end of the world, and were to die long before the remission of sins had been preached to all nations.

We see then that by *you* our Lord meant the apostles and their successors, the priests of His Church to the end of time. As the Father sends Him, He sends them—to forgive sins in His name, with the promise that what they forgive He will forgive. Therefore, whenever the priest's absolution falls on sins that have been confessed and sorrowed for, our Lord Himself says as He said to the poor sick man at Capharnaum: "Be of good heart, thy sins are forgiven thee."

# III
# Preparation for Confession

Have you seen in one of the London omnibuses a picture of a doctor making a sick-call? He is feeling the pulse of his patient and telling him he is a little bit run down, but will soon be himself again if he takes his medicine properly.

This is what our Lord says to us now. He beckons us to Him tenderly and promises to make us well and strong again, no matter what we have done to hurt ourselves. "Come to Me, child, and I will put you right again." He promises. He does not say "perhaps." And so we do not *hope*, but *know for certain* that we shall be put right *if we do our part*. For the sacraments *always* give grace to those who receive them worthily. We come to Him, then, joyfully, asking Him to do His part, and promising to do ours which we know consists of four things:

I. **We must heartily pray for grace to make a good confession.**

II. **We must carefully examine our conscience.**

III. **We must take time and care to make a good act of contrition.**

IV. **We must resolve by the help of God to renounce our sins and to begin a new life for the future.**

◆

**I. We must pray for grace to make a good confession.**

Because this is an important work and we can do no good work without the help of God's grace. Because it is sometimes difficult to tell our sins. And because prayer is the means fixed by God for getting His help. "Ask," He says, "and you shall receive." You may say one of the hymns to the Holy Spirit, or:

## Prayer for Help

I believe that there, behind the tabernacle door, is the Judge of the living and the dead, before Whom I shall have to appear when I die, to give an exact account of my whole life. I believe that He will have to judge me then with strict justice, that there will be no time for confession and contrition then. O my Judge and my Saviour, now while I have time, help me to find out my sins and to confess them with true sorrow, that I may stand without fear before You in the terrible hour of Judgment.

Holy Mary, Mother of God, pray for me a sinner *now* and at the hour of my death.

◆

**II. We must carefully examine our conscience.**

If you go to confession frequently and examine your conscience every night, preparation for the Sacrament of Penance becomes very easy. You come to it with the work half done. Set to work briskly the minute you get into church, not dawdling over it, not wool- gathering, not looking about and wasting time in distractions, but beginning at once with the first of the four points. Follow some order in the arrangement of what you have to say—the ten commandments of God; the six precepts of the Church; the seven deadly sins; or—to cover the same ground in another way—your duties (1) to God; (2)

to your neighbour; (3) to yourself. Your sins will thus remain in your memory, and when your examination is finished you will be able to leave them quietly and turn to your next point. Without an orderly arrangement, examination of conscience becomes difficult and wearisome, and even when it is finished, you will be running after your sins instead of thinking how to get rid of them. Ten minutes given to it in a business-like way is enough for an ordinary confession. Give the rest of the time, another ten minutes, to your contrition.

When we have not been to confession for some time, and even in our preparation for our weekly confession, we may sometimes find it useful to recall the places we have been in, and the persons we have met. This helps us to remember our sins. Any circumstance that changes the kind of sin and makes it much worse, *e.g.*, striking a parent, stealing anything belonging to a church, must be mentioned; and as far as we can we should say the number of times a sin has been committed.

The care we are to give to our examination is to be a reasonable care, such as we should give to a matter of importance. The Catechism says we are to examine our conscience carefully. It does not say we are to *fidget* over it. Remember that this part of our preparation is not the only or chief part, and that after reasonable care has been given to it, a sin forgotten is forgiven. Again, do not worry yourself by thinking you have committed a mortal sin without knowing it. No one, as we have seen, could do this, because one of the things required to make a sin mortal is that we know quite well what we are doing. Try to strike a match or write a letter without knowing what you are about. When you can do this, and not till then, will you be able to commit a mortal sin without knowing it—and without remembering it too.

By the law of God we are bound to confess every mortal sin once, and be absolved for it once. We are not bound to confess our venial sins. But it is well to do so. A good practice is to pick out two or three of the chief and try to be sorry for them. This is better than spending much time in trying to remember them all.

# A Form of Examination of Conscience

## (I) Towards God.

**Confession.** How long is it since my last? Did I do the four things by way of preparation? Did I leave out anything I ought to have told? Did I take time and care to make a good act of contrition? What was my purpose of amendment like? Did I say my penance carefully?

**Communion.** Did I make the usual acts before and after? And how?

**Prayers.** When I kneel down to pray do I remember that I am going to speak to God, and make at least a good start? Do I say my prayers in a hurry, or looking about all the time? Have I said my morning and night prayers, and without willful distractions? Have I examined my conscience at night and made a real act of sorrow for my sins? Have I laughed or talked in church, or shown any irreverence during Mass or Benediction? Have I done anything to distract others at prayer? How do I listen to sermons or catechism? Have I said grace before and after meals as I ought?

Have I done or read anything likely to injure my faith?

Have I spoken with disrespect of God, or of holy things? Have I said bad words?

Have I stayed away from Mass on any Sunday or Holy day of Obligation? Have I been late on these days, or inattentive?

## (II) Towards my Neighbour.

Have I disobeyed parents, or any one else in authority over me? Have I provoked them, or shown disrespect in word or manner? Have I caused them great sorrow, or not helped them when they were poor, or old, or sick? Have I done what I was told at once, or been angry, or answered back? Have I been obstinate, sulky, or impertinent when told of my faults? Have I deceived my parents or those who are over me?

Have I been in a passion? or kept up bad temper for a long time? Have I struck any one or quarrelled? Have I called people names, or in other ways provoked them? Have I wished harm to anyone? Have I refused to forgive? Have I given bad example to anyone by word or conduct? Or shared in any sin by proposing it, defending it, or in any other way? Have I done anything to spite my parents, teachers, or companions?

Have I prevented others from studying, or working, or in any way doing their duty?

Have I given unnecessary trouble to parents or superiors?

Have I stolen anything, or kept what did not belong to me, without trying to find the owner? Have I destroyed, wasted, or wilfully damaged things? Have I paid back anything I owed?

Have I told lies, or got others to tell them? (A lie of excuse that does not harm another, is a venial sin.) Have I told any lie that I knew would be the cause of harm to another? (This is calumny, and *may* be a mortal sin.) Have I made known any one's secret faults? (This is detraction.) Have I injured my neighbour's character by speaking ill of him, or listened *willingly* to uncharitable conversation? Have I judged anyone rashly, that is, thought ill of him without sufficient cause? Have I made others quarrel, or made mischief by tale-bearing?

NOTE.—If I have sinned by calumny, detraction, or theft, I must repair as well as I can the harm I have done, and ask my confessor's advice how to do it.

## (III) Towards Myself.

Have I done anything wrong, by thought, word, or deed, against purity or modesty? Have I got others to do wrong? Have I gone with bad companions? Have I read bad books, or given them to others?

> NOTE I.—A bad thought which is not wilful is no sin, but not to try to put away the bad thought, to take pleasure in it, to consent to it—this is a sin.

> NOTE 2.—Tale-telling to make mischief, or out of spite is wrong. But if you know of any immodest conduct or conversation carried on, you must at once make it known to your parents, or those in authority, and not fear to be called "tell-tale." If you neglect to do this, you may become answerable for such sins by concealment.

Have I been vain of my abilities, my person, or my dress? Have I despised others? Have I been jealous of others, or vexed when my companions were praised?

Have I been greedy? Have I, without leave, eaten meat on Friday, or on any day when it is forbidden?

Do I rise promptly in the morning, or am I lazy?

Have I been idle at my lessons? Have I stayed away from school or kept others away?

Have I, through curiosity, read letters or anything I ought not to have read? What about the duties and occupations of my daily life—how have they been done—-conscientiously, or carelessly?

Have I done anything else that I ought to confess? What is my chief fault, from which most of the others come—pride, anger, sloth, or what? Am I trying to conquer it?

## Another Form of Examination of Conscience

**I. Duties to God.**

*What about—*
- Confession,
- Communion,
- Mass,
- Benediction,
- Morning and night prayers, with examination of conscience,
- Grace before and after meals,
- Holidays of Obligation,
- Days of fasting and abstinence,
- Speaking with reverence of God and all holy persons and things?

**II. Duties to my Neighbour.**

*What about—*
- Contempt, stubbornness, disobedience to parents and lawful superiors,
- Fighting, quarrelling, and injurious words,
- Giving scandal and bad example,
- Anger, hatred, and revenge,
- Sharing in any sin by provocation, consent, or silence,
- Unjust taking away or keeping what belongs to another,
- Cheating in buying or selling,

- Wasting master's time or property,
- False testimony, rash judgment, and lies,
- Calumny, detraction, tale-bearing?

### III. Duties to Myself.

*What about—*
- Pride as to gifts of body or mind, family, wealth, dress, &c.,
- Wasting time in overmuch novel-reading, recreation, or in other ways,
- Curiosity in reading dangerous books, or newspapers, or in any other way,
- Greediness?

Is there anything else I ought to confess, or as to which I want advice?

Think now of some sin of your past life for which you are specially sorry and which you intend to confess again. Make an act of contrition for it.

**My God, I am sorry for all the sins since my last confession, most of all for this one (***name it***) and for this sin of my past life (***name it***).**

You must not be vexed with me if I say once more—Do give yourself time after your examination of conscience to think quietly over the motives for contrition. It seems silly, I know, to insist so much on what is simple common sense. And it *would* be silly, if people always brought their common-sense with them to confession. But some of us seem to make a point of leaving it behind. Hence we have to be reminded of what is so plain and simple.

A person once said: "I have to help a friend to prepare in confession, and this is how I do it. I give him half an hour to get ready, and all that time I keep him hunting up and down for his sins. When he has got them together as well as he can and is trying to hold them fast, I frighten him by saying that some big ones have probably escaped him. This makes him very uneasy, and off he sets hunting again, coming back after a long search quite tired out, having found nothing, but very uneasy all the same. Then I make him more so. For as his turn for confession has come before he has had any time to think of his contrition or purpose of amendment, I send him into the confessional telling him he will probably make a bad one for want of sorrow. In short, I do my utmost to turn the sacrament of mercy into a sacrament of misery for him."

Who would own to cruelty such as this? Yet it is thus some of us treat our own poor souls. *I* have some one to prepare as often as my day for confession comes round. How do I treat that some one? Cruelly, like this? If so, let me ask myself what right I have to do that harm to my own soul, which I should tremble to do to the soul of another.

Examinations are necessary things. At least we take this for granted now-a-days. But who likes them for their own sake? Once over, how gladly we turn away from them to something else—as we are going to do now.

◆

### III. We must take time and care to make a good act of contrition.

This is the chief part of our preparation, without which all the rest is worse than useless. Have we gathered together every sin we have committed?—not one will be forgiven without contrition. And on the other hand, should any sin, even a grievous one, be forgotten after sufficient care, our act of contrition, which would include that and every other grievous sin if we remembered it, would blot it out.

Now what is this contrition that we must have? The

catechism says it is "a hearty sorrow for our sins, because by them we have offended so good a God, together with a firm purpose of amendment." Notice that true sorrow looks two ways—backwards, to hate sin in the past; and forwards, to avoid it in the future.

We can be sorry for our sins for many reasons—for having brought upon us a public reproof, or deprived us of some enjoyment, or annoyed a friend. This is natural sorrow, and no matter how hearty it may be, it is of no use whatever for obtaining pardon of our sins. But if the friend we are sorry to have offended be God, or the enjoyment lost be heaven, or the reproof be hell—then our sorrow is *supernatural*, that is, proceeding from a motive suggested by faith, and this helped by the grace of God is sufficient for forgiveness.

The best motive for sorrow is God Himself—to be sorry for God's sake, because He is infinitely good and deserving of all love, and because by sin we have displeased and disappointed Him Whom we love. This perfect contrition is so pleasing to God, that it gets forgiveness at once for all guilt, mortal or venial, even before confession and absolution. If sufficiently intense, it remits all punishment too, eternal and temporal. It remits more or less, according to our dispositions. Imperfect contrition, called also attrition, is supernatural sorrow, but chiefly for our own sake, because we have lost heaven, or deserved hell or purgatory. Though less perfect than the other, it is good and put into our hearts by the Holy Ghost. It will forgive venial sin and remit a part of the temporal punishment, and is sufficient when joined with confession and absolution for the forgiveness of mortal sin.

Besides being supernatural, sorrow for sin must be *interior*, that is, coming from the heart. Mere words or outward signs would be useless; we must want and mean to be sorry. Sorrow must also be *supreme*. We must hate mortal sin above all other evils. Not that we must *feel* more sorrow than for other evils, the death of a father or mother, for instance. But in our minds we must judge it to be really the worst of evils, and we must be resolved never to commit a mortal sin for the love or fear of anything whatsoever. Lastly, our sorrow must be *universal*, including all mortal sin. One mortal sin not repented of stops the forgiveness of all others and shows our sorrow for others to be false. God cannot forgive some mortal sins and leave others unforgiven. If we confess venial sins only, we must be sorry for at least one. For all, if we want them to be forgiven by the sacrament.

God cannot forgive any sin, mortal or venial, without contrition. It is part of the matter of the sacrament, and we are bound to take it with us whenever we go to confession. To make sure of our contrition, it is well to tell some sin of our past life for which we are truly sorry and have *renewed our act of contrition*. We tell it, not of course to get it forgiven, that was done long ago, but simply because of the obligation to have sorrow for at least one sin that we confess. Hence, to tell it merely through habit and without having renewed our sorrow for it, is of no use whatever.

See how necessary contrition is, it almost seems to be the one thing necessary. We simply *must have it*. Like Saul standing a head and shoulders above his brethren, it over-tops everything else. Now how are we to get it? The catechism says "by earnestly praying for it, and by making use of such considerations as may lead us to it." Not a word about *feelings*, notice. For this reason, that these are out of our reach. If God gives us a strong feeling of sorrow, or even tears, we must thank Him heartily, most heartily, for it is a great grace. But it is not necessary, and He does not require it. God never asks of us anything which it is not in our power to give. The sorrow of our will is in our power; we can and must give it Him. Like all good things it must come from Him, but He has promised that all who ask shall receive and all who seek shall find. We will ask for it with all our heart, and we will seek for it by thinking over some of the things which will move us to it. Thinking, not scampering over, not merely reading, but letting our mind and heart go with the words we read. This is our part; if we do it, God will come in and do His.

**My God, give me true sorrow for having offended You. I must come to You for it. I cannot get it by myself. But I know You want to give it to me more than I want to have it. I know there is nothing You are so pleased to give. You tell me to ask and I shall receive, to seek and I shall find, to knock and it shall be opened to me. I am asking, seeking, knocking now. Give me what I want—perfect contrition for all my sins, sorrow for them because they have offended You Who are so good. Give me what I ask, through Jesus Christ our Lord.**

If we want to be sorry for our sins, we must think quietly of the motives or reasons why we should be sorry; we must try to find out how bad sin is. It takes some trouble to do this, well, we must take the trouble. Surely the great God of heaven and earth, Who, if He liked, might refuse to forgive us our sins, no matter how much trouble we took, or how sorry we were— does not ask too much when He bids us take ten minutes to find out the harm we have done ourselves and Him, and to be sorry for that harm. When Naaman, the general of the King of Syria, was told to wash seven times in the Jordan and he should be healed of his leprosy, he was vexed at having to do something so simple and easy. This childishness of his was too foolish for anything, and his very servants reproved him for it. "If the prophet had told thee to do some great thing." they said, "surely thou shouldst have done it. How much more when he bids thee only to wash seven times." Naaman took this advice well, washed, and was cured. If God had told us to do something very difficult—to fast on bread and water for a year, to do penances like the saints, we should have been obliged to do it, for we simply *must* get our sins forgiven. How much more are we obliged, and how grateful we ought to be to Him, when what He tells us to do is so light and easy.

Any thought that leads us to supernatural sorrow will serve our purpose, and if one is enough we need not use more. Some unexpected joy has come to you this week and made you feel what a good Father you have in heaven. Use this goodness of God as a motive for being heartily ashamed of yourself for having treated Him so badly, heartily sorry for having repaid Him so ungratefully.

Or you may think how dreadful a thing sin is in itself; of the dismal effects of mortal sin—how it kills the soul and deserves hell. To understand how it can kill what is immortal, you must understand that the soul has two lives—a natural life and a supernatural. The natural life is that which it receives when it is created, and which it will never lose. It is of this life the catechism speaks when it says: "My soul can never die." The supernatural life of the soul consists in the possession of the grace of God. Mortal sin kills the soul by depriving it of this super-natural life, without which it is dead in the sight of God.

Mortal sin also takes away the merit of our past good works, that is, it makes us lose the eternal reward gained by all the good works we have done in a state of grace. Moreover, it prevents any good work we may do whilst in a state of mortal sin from meriting an eternal reward. Only God's friends can gain merit for heaven, and we are made His enemies by mortal sin. If by the mercy of God we recover His friendship by grace, our past merits are restored to us, but the works done whilst in the miserable state of sin are works lost for eternity. Should not these thoughts make us fear and hate sin above all other evils?

Here are some other motives:—

I must hate sin because God hates it. He hates it
* *Because sin hurts me.* A good father is angry with any one or anything that harms his child. God sees how sin harms me, and because He is so fond of me, He hates it.

Let us see how sin hurts me. Have you ever heard of the god Moloch, and how he used to be worshipped by the sacrifice of the most precious treasures his worshippers possessed—their little children? The parents brought them to the place where, surrounded by a great fire, the hideous idol stood, holding out its arms. Into those iron arms the dear living babies were put. The arms fell and dropped them into the flames below. It was the devil who suggested these sacrifices. Think how horribly cruel he must be to have found pleasure in all that pain to fathers and mothers, as well as to the poor little victims themselves! The devil is through and through—*cruel.* Now if there is anything that shows a thoroughly bad nature it is cruelty. This is why a good father or mother will punish a child severely for taking pleasure in hurting a kitten or a fly. They want to stop in good time the growth of a passion which would make their child grow up a perfect monster, hateful to God and man.

The devil is a monster of cruelty as we see by the way in which he treated the poor possessed people brought to our Lord for cure. But it is only in hell that he can be as cruel as he likes. God's hand stays him here. He cannot do us here all the harm he would like. But once in hell, he has his victims safe. Those doors will never open to let them out. His time is come. He may treat them there just as he likes—and that for ever! But how is he to bring us to those gates? There is only one way—*by sin.* All sins, even little ones, lead that way. They may be a long way off, some of them, but they bring us nearer and nearer. Walking along the highway we come across a mile-stone: "8 miles from Whitby." We go on chatting and talking and come upon another stone: "5 miles from Whitby." On again, and on. Another stone: "2 miles from Whitby." We shall get there if we go on long enough. So it is on the road of sin. Any passion, any bad habit—curiosity, lying, bad temper, greediness—if left unchecked, may easily bring me to hell. This is why God hates sin, all sin—because of the harm it does me, the terrible danger in which it puts me of losing my soul.

◆ Again, God hates sin *because it deceives me.* Nothing makes a father so angry as to see his child deceived. He will use severe words to a servant whom he finds tricking even a baby. Now sin tricks us. It looks such a little thing that I can scarcely believe it can do me much harm. I do not see how the small worm among the petals of the rosebud is quietly eating them away and ruining what is so fair. I do not know of the rotten plank carried by the splendid ship now starting on her course, and how after years at sea, it will give way beneath the constant pressure of the waves and sink her with all on board. God sees in my soul the hidden passion which will be my ruin unless I pluck it out whilst I am still young. He knows the weak part of my soul, and how when temptation presses there will be sin, unless I am on my guard and strengthen myself in time.

◆ Again, *sin spoils me.* God loves what is beautiful. His world is full of beauty. Beauty falls from His hand when-ever He opens it. But of all the fair things He has made, none is so fair as the soul of the little child in its baptismal innocence. He loves it. He tries to keep it safe, as we put our hands over a pet plant that some one is trying to snatch and spoil.

Even if sin should not cause the death of my soul, it disfigures it in the eyes of God. Therefore He hates it. Lying, greediness, anger, may not take away its life, but they really injure it. Can we bear to see that injured which we care for very much? In vain does the doctor try to console the poor father whose little child is lying sick upstairs. She is not going to die, it is true, but the ugly disease which has covered her face will disfigure it terribly, and her father cannot be comforted. God loves us more, oh a thousand times more than the tenderest father ever loved his pet child. And He cannot bear sin, the frightful disease of the soul, that spoils it in His sight.

♦ God hates sin *because of the evil fruit it bears*. There is a law that harvests must correspond with sowing. If we sow corn we shall reap corn. If we sow weeds we must reap weeds. This is why God is so anxious we should not let bad seeds have time to sink into our souls; why He has left the confessional open, not only now and then, but practically at all times. He says to us: "I know you cannot keep from all sin because you are weak, but do not remain in sin; do not let bad seed take root and spread its fibres through your soul; do not let its poison soak in through and through." A boy sows an acorn when he is a mere baby of four. Years pass and the acorn grows but slowly. He could pull it up easily. But let it grow with his growth till he is a man, and he will only be able with difficulty to uproot it. So it is with a bad passion suffered to grow in our soul.

God does not want us to have all this pain. Therefore He bids us watch our souls to see what we are casting into them, pluck up weeds as soon as they show themselves, and thus leave Him good soil and plenty of room in which to sow His own good seed.

♦ God hates sin *because of its ingratitude*. This is a vice we all detest, and so heartily that it is a satisfaction to us to see it punished as it deserves. We can bear to be reproached for anything sooner than for this: "Whatever I may be, I am not ungrateful to those who are good to me," we say. But are we so sure of this? Or is God out of count because His goodness is past all reckoning, stretching over all my life and every hour of my life; because He has given me all the good things I have, and is ready to give me presently all I can desire?  Let me put into one scale all that God has done for me, and into the other all I have done for Him in return.

In one scale my creation, my redemption, and all redemption means. That the Son of God became a child for me, and a poor child, living as the children of the poor live, without comforts, often without necessaries. That when He grew up, He spent long years toiling, teaching, suffering for my sake. That He died for me at last the cruellest of deaths.  That He has put all the merits of His Life and Passion into the Sacraments to give grace to my soul through them.  That He is this hour preparing my place in heaven, and at the same time is shut up in the tabernacle to be my Friend, to Whom I may run in every trouble. This is how God proves His love for me.

In the other scale I put my proofs of love for Him.  What are they?...Have I at least shown myself thankful to Him?  Or must I own that I have been ungrateful to the best of fathers, unfaithful to the truest of friends?

**My God, there is no help for it. I must own myself guilty of what I detest with all my heart—the shameful sin of ingratitude. I cannot excuse myself. I have repaid Your love with the sins of my past life, with those I am bringing now to Your feet. This is the weight I have put into the scale. O my Father and my Friend, I am very sorry for all my sins, most of all for the ingratitude that troubled You so much as to make You sorrowful even unto death.**

Or take any thoughts about hell, purgatory, heaven, the sufferings of Christ, the goodness of God.  You need not use all, some will help you at one time, some at another.

### I. Hell

"Eye hath not seen, nor ear heard, neither hath it entered

into the heart of man what things God hath prepared for those that love Him." (I Cor. 2.) Yes, and on the other hand—eye hath not seen, nor ear heard, nor can we have any idea of what is prepared after death for those who have not loved Him, who die His enemies by mortal sin. The judgment is swiftly over, and before the friends on earth know that the soul has left the body, it has gone to its place in hell, and begun its eternity of misery. The exact nature of its pain we do not know, but this we know, that our Lord always speaks of the punishment of that fearful place as *fire*. "*The wicked shall be cast into the furnace of fire.*" (Matt. 13.) "*Depart from Me, you cursed, into everlasting fire.*" (Matt. 25.)

Fire! Is there any word which makes the heart leap with terror like that word? We shudder at the horrors of a railway accident, at the wounds inflicted in the awful warfare of these days, at the sufferings caused by plague, famine, earthquake, floods. But nothing of all this horrifies us like the pain of burning. We have all perhaps felt in some tiny way what this pain is like. A slight scald or burn has caused us almost unbearable pain. Anyhow, we are all agreed, from the strong man to the tiny child, that no pain is to be dreaded like the pain of fire.

Our Lord does not like to frighten us. He came amongst us as a little babe that He might not frighten us. He hides His glory in the Blessed Sacrament lest we should be afraid and stay away from Him. He was always saying to His friends: "Fear not." But there is something He does want to frighten us about—Hell. He wants to fill us all with this fear—good and bad, His friends and His enemies, the old man and the little child.

We think it is cruel to frighten a child. But was it cruel of the mother who found her baby getting inside the fender, to hold its little hand to the fire till it began to cry out? There was no more going too near the fire after that.

Our Lord wants to frighten us about hell-fire *now* when the fear will do us good, that we may not come to fear it when fear will be too late. And so there are no words more fearful than the words about hell that fell from His gentle lips. "I am tormented *in this flame*," He makes the rich man say. "Every one shall be *salted with fire*." "*And the fire is not extinguished.*" "If thy eye scandalize thee cut it off, it is better for thee to enter into life, maimed, than having two hands to go into hell *into unquenchable fire*." (Mark 9.) Fire—how He repeats again and again that dreadful word! He wants to show us that we must wrench ourselves free from books, amusements, companions—things near and dear to us as hand or foot, rather than do anything to deserve the awful punishment of the life to come.

And who are these that He wants to warn? Bad people only who have no fear of mortal sin? No, but those too who are getting careless about venial sin, who say, "Oh, it is only a venial sin." He showed St. Teresa the place in hell prepared for her if she had not corrected a certain fault. The greatest saints must be afraid of hell. "I say to you, my friends, fear Him Who has power to cast into hell." St. Paul was afraid, St. Philip Neri was afraid. The catechism says hell is one of the Four Last Things to be ever remembered. Why? That we may all be afraid.

"The *place* of *torments*." Pain of every kind there. Pain most awful in its severity. Pain never ceasing; always at a pitch of unbearable intensity; never a little less bad; never soothed by hearing a kind word; never relieved by the least comfort, the least change. Pain without merit; of no good to the wretched soul; not getting rid of its guilt; not bringing it any nearer to the end of its punishment. Pain such as this, unbearable from the first moment, to go on—*for ever!*

In bed with a feverish cold for a few days, how slowly time passes, how long the days seem, how endless the nights! What would it be if this confinement were to be, not for a few days, but for months, for years! "O doctor," you would say, "how long is this to last? When shall I be up and out again?"

What must it be to be imprisoned, not in a comfort-able bed at home, with father and mother, brothers and sisters coming in and out. But to be all alone in the dark prison of hell—and that, not for years, but—*for ever!*

Think too of the company there. If you would not for anything in the world be locked up for one night with a madman, or even with a dead body, how could you bear to be shut up for ever in the darkness of hell with the devils whose very name freezes you with horror—all their rage let loose upon you, no one standing by to stop their cruelty.

The pain of which our dear Lord speaks, whatever its nature may be, reaches the *soul*. How, we do not know. But we know that the pain it causes is more terrible by far than any pain of fire the body can suffer. And even this pain is nothing compared with that which makes hell what it is—the pain of loss. Until we know Who God is, as He is known by all in the next world, we cannot under-stand in the very least what the soul feels that has lost Him.

The pain of loss is like an eternal suffocation. God is to our souls in the next life what air is to our bodies in this. They cannot live without it; they struggle frantically to get it. So it is with every soul in the next world, the bad as well as the good, those who hate God as well as those who love Him—He is the life of all. The good have gained everything in gaining Him. In losing Him, the wicked have lost *all*. "My God and my all!" the saints exclaim in transports of joy. "Let me get to God," the damned cry out in their suffocating agony, "I must, I will have Him." They leap up each moment to reach Him, and each moment fall back into the fire, wailing in their despair: "O God, Whom I might have loved—*my God* once, *my God* still—I have lost You, I have lost You for ever, I have lost all—and by my own fault!"

> One moment—God's beloved child,
>     Heir to a throne,
> Saints, Angels, Mary, God Himself,
>     By right, mine own.
>
> Another moment—mine by right,
>     A felon's cell,
> Companionship of demons, and
>     The doom of hell!

Here is one of the most unbearable thoughts in hell, that place of bitter thoughts: "*It is all my own fault!* I need not have given way to temptation. I should not have given way if I had prayed. I am lost, and for what? How long did the pleasure of a mortal sin last? I am lost for so little, lost when I might so easily have been saved! And now it is too late!" This thought those miserable souls have always before them—*It is too late!* What did the bad thief think of the choice he had made, when he found himself in hell, and knew that his companion of a few moments ago was in paradise with Jesus!

Is it not a fearful thought that I may be lost and go to hell! Must I not hate and keep away from mortal sin, and be afraid of venial sin! For I must remember that hell is not to punish sin in general, but *my* sins if I should die in mortal sin. "I am tormented in this flame!" is the cry, not of Dives only, but of every one who falls into that furnace of fire. It would be *my* cry if I were to die in mortal sin.

But some one may say: "I will be sorry afterwards, and go to confession and put all right." Setting aside the horrible ingratitude of such a speech, look at its madness, for it means: "I know God has forbidden this sin under pain of losing my soul. I know He is all powerful and can do with me what He wills. I know that in the moment in which I offend Him, He can snap the thread of my life and let me drop into unquenchable fire. But I don't care. I will brave His power. I will insult Him to His Face. Then, *if He spares me* and gives me contrition and time to go to confession, I shall be all right again and none the worse for having run such a risk."

"Be not deceived. God is not mocked." How often death has come suddenly, before contrition, before confession; and from its place in hell the miserable soul has looked back upon that risk it ran five minutes ago, and learnt to its cost what it is to mock the mercy of God.

We measure a crime by its punishment. If a man is fined a few shillings, his offence we say must have been light. If he is sentenced to penal servitude for life, he must have done something very wrong. If we hear he is to be hanged or shot, he must be a murderer or a traitor.

So we may measure sin. How dreadful that offence must be which God punishes with *death!* He is infinitely just. He cannot be too severe and punish overmuch. He is infinitely good, and kind, and loving. He has done all He could for that soul just condemned to eternal torments. He made it to be happy with Him for ever. He loved it dearly. He gave His only Son for its salvation. He adopted it as His child, and made a place ready for it in heaven. Oh, what a horrible thing that must be to cause a child of God and heir of heaven to be thrust down from its throne into the prison-house of hell!

> Father, I tremble lest temptation's power
>     Make me forget the place
> Prepared for me—awaiting me this hour,
>     Before Thine unveiled Face;
>
> Give me Thy love; but if that love should fail
>     Passion's fierce storm to quell,

> Then let Thy dreadful chastisements avail
>> To save my soul from hell.
>
> Let me lose all, my Father and my Friend,
>> So Thou to me remain,
> So I but safely reach Thee in the end
>> And life eternal gain.

## 2. Purgatory

Many people are more helped by the thought of purgatory than by that of hell. They find purgatory teaches them more about the malice of sin and makes them fear and hate it more. Let us see why.

The souls suffering in hell are the enemies of God. The holy souls in purgatory are His friends and dear children. They love Him with all their strength, and He loves them more tenderly than the fondest mother ever loved her child. Yet see how He is obliged to treat them, because, though their sins are forgiven, the debt of temporal punishment remains.

The consequences of our sins do not end, as some of us seem to think, with the confession of them. Sin and punishment go together like a burn and pain. The first sacrament we receive takes away the pain with the sin, but the Sacrament of Penance leaves a punishment behind. Your father said to you once: "Well, it is the first time you have been disobedient, so I will forgive you." But the next time, though he forgave you, there was punishment. This is God's way, as we see by the chastisements that came upon Moses and David. These were terrible, but nothing to the chastisements of the next life. We must try to bring home to ourselves the pain of the punishment of sin in purgatory.

A great singer was once summoned by a King to take part in a grand musical festival to be given at the palace. Everything was provided for his journey, but through his own carelessness he arrived late, and was shut out. Standing in the dark under the walls, he caught, faint and broken, the grand strains within as they rose and fell. The harmony, though entrancing, was imperfect—his part throughout was wanting. Oh, how he longed to be there and have his share. How bitterly he bewailed his negligence—but too late!

So is it with the souls that through their own fault are excluded for awhile from the eternal festival. They hear from afar the songs of the blessed, but their part is missing. The chorus is arranged for their voices; they should be joining in that glorious praise. But by their own fault they are shut out.

When a soul in sanctifying grace appears before our Lord for judgment, He opens His arms and welcomes it to its Home. He says to it: "Come, blessed of My Father, possess the Kingdom prepared for you from the foundation of the world." And then—how sadly, "My child, I should be so glad to let you come to Me at once, but those venial sins of yours, those daily faults done with full knowledge that they were displeasing to Me, have made a great debt against you, and you will have to go to the prison-house till all is paid."

Oh, the agony of that poor soul then!—not so much because of the dark prison to which it is condemned, as because it must go away from Him Whom it loves. It has seen His Face, it has seen His smile, and—it must go away. It pines with an intensity of which we can form no conception, to see that Face always, to be with Him, to enjoy Him, to hold Him fast, to have Him for its own for ever. It knows now that it can never be happy but with Him—and it has to be banished far from Him. We shall never understand the anguish caused by its love till we come to be ourselves in its place. The intense love of God is what makes purgatory so terrible. A child when it sees its mother, springs towards her. It struggles with those who would hold it back. It holds out its arms to be taken into hers. It cries, it sobs, nothing will comfort it till she takes it up and clasps it to her breast. So is it with the soul that longs for God. All other pains are nothing to the loss of God.

A report was afloat in the autumn of 1899, to the effect that the end of the world would come on November 13th of that year. The subject happened to be mentioned by a gentleman in a house where there were several little children, and was discussed in their hearing.

On the evening of November 12th, nurse was alarmed by a noise in the night-nursery, and hastening thither, found Lil sobbing hard. Mother had said the end of the world would be to-morrow, and mother was going to London...and...and...Lil would have to be burnt up...*without her!* Of course mother was by the side of the cot directly, but it was some time before the little one could be soothed and comforted and coaxed to go to sleep.

Notice it was not the being burnt up, but the being burnt up *without mother* that was so dreadful. In the mind of even a very little child there is an idea of pain worse by far than any that hurts the body. It helps us to understand something of the pain of loss.

Purgatory is a dark close prison. The exact nature of the sufferings there we do not know, but Holy Scripture says some "shall be saved yet so as by fire" (1 Cor. 3), and the greatest saints tell us that the least pain there is worse than anything that can be suffered in this world. No words can tell what the poor prisoners endure. They have nothing to do but to suffer intense and unceasing pain, without being able to help themselves in the least. What would violent toothache be for a week together! The pains of purgatory have to be borne for months, years, perhaps centuries. Should not this thought make us tremble! If I am careless about venial sin, how long I may have to be there!

From their terrible prison-house these souls cry to God, "Open to us, O Lord, open to us!" Oh, how they hate now the venial sins of which they thought so little once. The irreverence in church; the wilful distractions in prayer; the unkindness to others in thought, and word, and deed; the impatience when things were not to their liking; the disobedience and disrespect to parents; the bad example to companions. "Oh, how foolish we were," they will cry, "not to believe what we were told—that venial sin is not a little evil, but the greatest in the world after mortal sin. If only we had remembered when we were tempted, that though God is good and easily forgives sin, yet the punishment remains—that each venial sin has its distinct debt of punishment to be paid either on earth or in purgatory! The angels and saints are longing for our company—and we may not join them. They are calling us to come and take our part in their songs of praise—and we can answer only by our sighs. We might have been there long ago, and here we must stay, perhaps for ages—all through our own fault. Bitterly, bitterly we say now what we often said unthinkingly on earth, "through my fault, through my fault, through my most grievous fault."

What makes the lot of these poor souls still harder, is the thought that they will gain nothing by all their patient suffering. The time for merit is past. They have simply to bear their pain till the last farthing of their debt is paid, and at the end will have deserved no higher place in heaven, and no nearer and clearer sight of God.

Yet purgatory, terrible as it is, is an invention of God's mercy. We owe it to His pitying kindness that there should be such a place. "Do you know, I think purgatory is a splendid contrivance," said a little child at catechism, "because we're not fit to go straight to heaven and we can't go to hell." She was right, but what must be the malice of sin which constrains God to invent such a place for undoing the harm sin has done, and makes such an invention an act of Divine generosity on His part!

"There are people who think God has a hard heart," said the holy Curé d'Ars. "Oh, how much they are mistaken. For He has given to His Son the tenderest of hearts, and no one can give what he has not himself."

It is we who are hard-hearted towards Him and towards ourselves. When we commit venial sin we force God to punish, not His enemies but His friends; to banish from His presence, not His servants but His children. Why should we make Him do what is so contrary to His love? He does so want to have us with Him in heaven, and give us all He has ready for us there. And we hold His hands. Instead of having us round Him, rejoicing in the brightness of His dear presence, He has to keep us shut out in the darkness, far away from our home.

To come now to myself. What venial sins this past week will have to be punished by the grievous pains of purgatory, unless I do a little willing penance for them here? What venial sins must I avoid in future, to prevent my debt of punishment from growing heavier? Once inside those gates, my sorrow and good resolutions will be too late. Our Lord will say to me: "The night has come, in which no man can work. I tell thee thou canst not go hence till thou hast paid the last farthing."

> Lord, let me come to Thee in joyful haste,
>   When life is done;
> I cannot wait whilst long and dreary years
>   In exile run;
> Pain there must be, for my so many sins,
>   Deserved disgrace;
> But quickly let it come and go—and then
>   Show me Thy Face.

## Our Heavenly Home

Oh the pleasant sights and sounds that come up before us when we say the word "Home!"—the favourite nooks, the delightful rambles, the dear fireside, the faces of brothers and sisters, the familiar voices, the freedom, the fun, the laughter. And, before and above all, all in two words—father and mother!

"What is home?" a teacher asked.

"Where mother is," answered a little child.

And our Heavenly Home, what is that? Is it as many seem to imagine, mere freedom from pain, and sickness, and sorrow, and death—a life without strife or care, without a moment's weariness or disquiet—and that for ever? It is this, but much more than this.

It is the possession of every joy that our wildest dreams can picture, joys of which God Himself can only speak as, "The good things of the Lord in the land of the living." (Ps. 26.)

It is to live in close and loving familiarity with angels and saints, our brothers and sisters in the Kingdom of God.

It is to kneel at Mary's feet; to look up into her face; to hear her words of love; to feel the touch of her motherly hand.

It is to be for ever in the company of Jesus, among His dear and chosen friends; seeing Him always; hearing His voice; receiving the marks of His love, and loving Him ourselves with every power of heart and soul.

It is to behold the unveiled Face of God; to know and love and praise with unspeakable delight, the Father, Son, and Holy Ghost, who created, redeemed, and sanctified us, and made us for heaven and for Himself. This is the joy that eye hath not seen, nor ear heard, nor heart conceived; the joy in which is all other joys; the joy that will satisfy to the full every desire of the heart, and that for eternity. Home is where our Father is, and therefore Heaven is Home.

This joy is the birthright of every baptized soul. It is my right. A place in my Father's house has been pre-pared for me. It is known there as mine, my name is written over it in letters of light.

> O Paradise, O Paradise,
> I greatly long to see
> The special place my dearest Lord
> Is furnishing for me.
> (*Faber.*)

But if ever I have committed a mortal sin, what have I done? Thrown away my title-deeds to that place; despised it; consented never to see it. "I cannot have it and the passing pleasure of this mortal sin," I have said. "Well, let it go. God may give it to another, for all I care. I will exchange it for a place in the outer darkness, where there is weeping and gnashing of teeth."

Angels and saints heard me and trembled. What if God should take me at my word? And why not? Why should my place in heaven be kept for me? *Thou hast lifted thyself up against the Lord of heaven, the God that hath thy breath in His hand.* (Dan. 5.) They trembled; they waited. But why were not their swords unsheathed against me? Why was not their eager zeal for God's glory let loose to sweep me from off the earth into the place I had chosen? Why were they thus patient with me? Because they always see the face of my Father who is in heaven. And they saw pity there. The Lord of heaven is my Father—and He had patience. He would not take me at my word. He would wait and call me back to Him, and give me grace, and restore to me all I had lost, if only I would be sorry, and let the Blood of Jesus flowing in the Sacrament of Penance make good my losses and win back for me my place at Home.

A prodigal, I hie me home,
My raiment rent, defiled;
Father, I am not worthy now
That Thou shouldst call me "child."

What shall I ask—a servant's lot,
A servant's work and hire?
More this than I deserve—but oh!
Give me what I desire:

Call me Thy child once more—my place,
My life at home with Thee;
Thy love, Thy smile, the kiss of old,
All this restore to me!

## Heaven lost

Hast thou lost Heaven?  Hast thou in madness cast
Thy birthright from thee, for a pleasure, past
Ere thou couldst grasp it?  Is thy throne by right,
That bore thy name in characters of light,
   Bartered away?

And art thou Esau-like bemoaning sore
What thou mayst wreck indeed but not restore—
A glorious purpose by thy folly crossed,
A Heaven within thy grasp, a Heaven lost,
   And lost for aye?

O foolish one, weep on—yet not in vain,
Thy Father calls thee to His arms again;
Rights by sin forfeited shall grace revive;
Heaven be thy portion yet, so thou but strive
   As thou hast striven.

Though thou with Him couldst part, not He with thee;
Thine everlasting dwelling-place must be
Where, mid the spotless, in untold delight,
Thou, happy child, shall revel in His sight,
   Loved and forgiven.

## The Sacred Passion

It is good and useful to turn to hell and purgatory and heaven to find what we want—sorrow for our sins. The bee goes to any and to every flower that offers any prospect of gain. But she has her predilections. One bunch of mignonette is more to her than a whole field of buttercups.

And the Sacred Passion is more to us than all the universe beside. There, if anywhere, we shall learn what sin is, by what sin has done. There, if all other founts fail us, we shall draw the sorrow we are seeking. But not all at once. It needs patient study before it gives out its treasures. Above all, it needs the love that dwells on detail. The reason why we can look at our crucifix unmoved and unhelped, is the carelessness of our glance. If we had to copy what we saw, we should see more, because we should have to look closer, longer, more attentively. We ought to be like the bee on the mignonette, which rifles each floweret before passing on. There is great diligence, but no hurry. If we would imitate her when we kneel before our crucifix, passing slowly from wound to wound, we should find what we want before we had gone far.

And so with the other scenes of the Passion. We look upon them carelessly, as a whole. We try to grasp too much. If we would force ourselves now and then to stay before one single circumstance of our Lord's many pains, we should begin to understand something of what He suffered for us, and to grieve for the sins which cost Him so much to expiate.

Let us go to two or three of these scenes now, remembering that when, like the bee, we have found what we want, we are *to stay there*, leaving the remaining stores to be explored another day.

## The Scourging

"And Pilate calling together the chief priests, and the magistrates, and the people, said to them: You have presented unto me this man, as one that perverteth the people, and behold I, having examined Him before you, find no cause in Him… I will chastise Him therefore and release Him." (Luke 23.)

Did ever judge in any land dare to make so unrighteous a speech? Was there ever a school in which such a reason for punishing a boy could be given with safety? "I find him innocent, therefore I will chastise him!" And here was one of that nation in which the sense of justice was so strong—a Roman governor—in broad daylight—from his seat of judgment—the lictors, officers of justice, in attendance—in face of a whole people, and of strangers out of every nation under heaven—saying: "I find no fault in Him, therefore I will chastise Him."

O children, you whose blood tingles at the very suspicion of unfairness, what will you feel for One who was the victim of injustice such as this!

Look into His Heart and try to feel what He felt—He the judge of the living and the dead, He the holy and the just One, who has done no sin. For His was a human heart and the most sensitive of hearts. It smarted as ours smarts, under injustice and wrong. But He thought of me and of my sins which His chastisement was to expiate—and Jesus was silent. One word, and that unjust judge had been torn from his judgment-seat by an indignant people—but Jesus was silent. He loved me and delivered Himself for me. To what?

Let us see. Remember it is not enough to read, *we must see; we must feel.*

See then at the foot of the marble steps leading from the balcony of the governor's hall, a large court paved with reddish stones. At one end a low pillar, not more than two feet and a half in height, with an iron ring in the top. To this ring our Lord is fastened by His wrists, so that His Sacred body is painfully bent.

See those long lashes tipped with spikes of iron. They are the scourges. Handle them, and think how they will rend and bruise and tear to pieces when wielded by the strong arms of soldiers. Watch these cruel men as they gather round their victim, who stands, as we should, trembling and terrified, awaiting the first stroke.

Look for an instant into heaven, and see the amazement, and hear the silence there. Can it be that the shameful and degrading punishment reserved for slaves is to be endured by the only-begotten Son of God! He knows what is due to His Divine Person. Surely He will call upon His Father to save Him from this indignity, and ten legions of angels will be sent to His aid. But Jesus is silent. He knows what is due to Himself. But He knows too that the chastisement of our sins is fallen upon Him, and that by His bruises we are to be healed. The suffering of His innocent flesh is to atone for the indulgence of our sinful flesh. Because He loves me, He delivers Himself for me.

Look at the scene in the courtyard as the scourgers begin their cruel work. See how pitilessly, on back, and shoulders, and arms, their furious blows are dealt. The delicate skin becomes red and swollen, the Blood begins to trickle and flow down. Then the iron points falling thick and fast, tear the flesh, until the sacred body is one great wound. And still they go on striking—striking on the open wounds. The scourges and the ground are covered with fragments of His sacred flesh; the Blood streams down upon the pavement.

A whole hour of torture such as this! Five thousand stripes! No pity, no thought for Him, as the tired soldiers relieve one another. From the sole of the foot to the top of the head, there is no soundness in Him—wounds, and bruises, and swelling sores.

And all for me! Do I thoroughly understand this? I believe it, but have I ever tried to make it real to myself? If I had, I should surely hate my sins which have been so cruel, I should love Him who has loved me so much as to bear this willingly for me.

> Had I stood by, that day in Pilate's hall,
> And watched a whole long hour the scourges fall;
> Marked how that tender flesh they slashed and tore,
> Whilst wide and wider grew each ghastly sore;
> Could I have been so hard, so pitiless
> As not to share with Him His keen distress?
> But had I known that hour, it was *for me*
> He, the All-Holy, stood in agony,
> Trembling with pain in every nerve and limb—
> What would, what must my heart have said to Him?

### The Crowning with Thorns

The scourging over, our Lord is loosed from the pillar. See Him staggering feebly to find His clothes which the soldiers have thrown here and there. See Him trying with weak and trembling hands to lift the seamless robe over His head, and how the woollen tunic adheres to the raw wounds on every side. No pity, no help, no word of comfort from any. "I looked for one that would grieve together with me, but there was none, and for one that would comfort me, and I found none." (Ps. 68.)

Not only did He find none to pity Him, but a fresh torment, one especially invented for Him, was at hand. From the court of the scourging He is dragged into the barrack-yard.

"Then the soldiers of the Governor taking Jesus into the hall, gathered together unto Him the whole band, and stripping Him, they put a scarlet cloak about Him. And platting a crown of thorns, they put it upon His head, and a reed in His right hand. And bowing the knee before Him, they mocked Him, saying: Hail! King of the Jews. And spitting upon Him, they took the reed and struck His head." (St. Matt. 27.)

When He clothed Himself so painfully after the scourging, our Lord knew that almost immediately His garments would be stripped from His bleeding wounds, that He might be dressed up as a mock king for the amusement of the soldiers. Think of the agony of that stripping. If we have a gathered finger, mother must dress it herself. How we beg her to be careful, and how we cry out when in spite of her gentle handling and precautions, the bandage sticks to the sore place. He was one wound when the rough hands of His tormentors plucked the woollen garments from the quivering flesh! Are we right in saying that each point of the Passion is enough, more than enough, to fill us with horror for sin; amazement at the charity which undertook to suffer all that sin deserves; loving contrition for our own sins which cost our Lord so dear?

Jesus had been called the King of the Jews. The soldiers can get some sport out of this. They throw an old scarlet cloak on His shoulders, seat Him on a stone bench, and put His crown upon His head. Look at that crown. Feel it. A long spiny branch of brier, roughly plaited into a wreath—only roughly, for the soldiers must take care not to hurt their hands with the thorns, which in Palestine are longer, sharper, and much stronger than any we have over here. They take this crown, put it on His head, and, lest it should fall off, beat it down with their sticks. The thorns pierce His head on every side. Through His hair the blood trickles down in many streams over His forehead, and with the rush of tears caused by the awful pain, fills His eyes and blinds them. See His noble brow covered with blood. His beautiful face on which the angels desire to look, all spoilt and disfigured. His eyes not knowing where to turn in their intolerable agony. Think how He fixes them on you, and asks you if you are not sorry for your share in bringing Him to this.

It was for our evil thoughts He suffered in His head. For our vanity that His beautiful face was disfigured, and His eyes were filled with blood.

> Was it my hand, O King of kings,
>   That wove that crown,
> And laid it on Thy royal head,
>   And pressed it down,
> Blinding with tears and trickling blood
>   Thine eyes divine,
> My God, was this the work of sin,
>   And sin of mine?

"And they began to salute Him: Hail! King of the Jews! And they struck His head with a reed. And they did spit on Him. And bowing their knees they adored Him." (St. Mark 15.)

Our Lord spoke very little of His sufferings. When they were near at hand, and He had to prepare His Apostles for them lest their faith in Him should fail utterly, He simply said: "The Son of Man shall be betrayed (Matt. 20) and delivered to the Gentiles, and shall be mocked and scourged, and spit upon, and put to death." (St. Luke 18.) These pains were nothing like all He had to suffer, but from His singling them out from the rest, we may gather that He counted them among the chief. Now we notice that of these six pains, four do not hurt the body. Think then what our Lord must have felt in that tender Heart of His. He loved His apostles dearly. They were His chosen friends, to whom He told His secrets, and He did so feel it, that one *of them* should turn against Him and betray Him to His enemies. He felt the ingratitude of His own people the Jews—that they to whom He had been promised so long, should deliver Him to the Gentiles to be put to death. He is the King of glory, the Lord of heaven and earth. In heaven thousands of thousands stand before Him, and ten thousand times a hundred thousand minister to Him. How He felt the mockery of His royalty on earth, when they "saluted Him... and bowing their knees adored Him." "And they did spit on Him"—on Him before whom the angels veil their faces and sing: "Holy, Holy, Holy." Yes, terrible as was the agony His delicate body suffered, the anguish of His shrinking, sensitive soul was worse by far.

See how in one mystery we may pass from pain to pain to feed our loving sorrow. This third among the sorrowful mysteries seems to be a favourite with children. Ask them to which of the scenes in the Passion they go by preference to gather sorrow for their sins, and you will hear again and again: "Oh, to the crowning with thorns."

### Christ crowned

Oh spare His Head, for He is King of kings,
The Lord our God, whose praise for ever rings
    Through the bright courts on high!
Shall thorns that venerable Head surround,
Shall "Christ the King" thus cruelly be crowned
    By earthly loyalty?

Oh spare the Face that angels veiled adore!
Mar not its beauty, nor defile it sore
    With pitiless disgrace:
All else hath been delivered to thy will,
Nor even this doth He withhold—yet still,
    Spare, spare that sacred Face!

Oh spare His Heart! Behold Him bruised and torn;
What man may bear and live, He now hath borne,
    And freely borne for thee:
For thee a heavy ransom He hath paid;
Bruises and swelling sores thy hand hath made,
    Oh spare Him mockery!

## Calvary

And now let us climb Mount Calvary and stand beneath the cross, as we might have stood that Friday afternoon long ago. The darkness and stillness of night is all around. Roman soldiers, Jewish priests, the scoffing Pharisees, the rabble, have been frightened into silence. Look at Him as He hangs there, so white against the blackness, so still in His awful agony. Look at Him, and see how "from the sole of the foot to the top of the head there is no soundness in Him, wounds and bruises and swelling sores." (Isaias i.) The bleeding hands and feet arrest our attention, and rightly. Yet we must not forget that in this, the last scene of torture, the pains of every other are renewed, and grow worse instead of lessening as the hours drag on.

Look at His head. For four hours it has borne its cruel crown, a crown so often snatched off and put on again, so knocked about when He fell, that the wounds it has made now number many hundreds. He has nowhere to rest this aching head. If He leans it against the cross, the thorns are forced in deeper; if He lets it hang forward upon His breast, the strain upon His hands becomes more intolerable.

See that pale, disfigured face; the bruised, sunken cheeks; the parched lips; the eyes growing glazed and dim. "There is no beauty in Him, nor comeliness,...no sightliness that we should be desirous of Him." (Isaias 53.) And He was the most beautiful of the children of men!

Each moment the nails driven into those delicate hands and feet tear wider and wider the rent they have made. The wounds of the scourging are smarting in the cold wind. The whole frame is quivering in its unbearable agony. At ease on a soft bed, we cannot remain long without turning. What was it to be stretched for three hours, raw and bleeding as He was, on the hard, knotty wood of the cross! We shudder at the thought of a limb out of joint. What must it have been to hang for three hours on those disjointed arms! We count it a hardship to be thirsty on a hot day. What was the fierceness of the thirst which broke the silence of those uncomplaining lips!

And the sufferings of His soul! Pitied by none in that immense crowd. Only words of mockery and hatred rising before His cross. Only gall and vinegar lifted to His lips. Only four or five friends true to Him, out of all the hundreds He had healed and helped. And those few faithful ones, so far from being able to comfort Him, sorely needing comfort themselves. In His own unutterable anguish and desolation He has to think of them, to provide for them.

All He possesses on earth, His few poor clothes, are taken from Him and divided among the soldiers. He has nothing left to Him in the world. He lifts His eyes above the world. He seeks the Father's face—the Father whose will He has done so perfectly, so perseveringly—to whom He has been obedient from His first breath in the manger to this death of the cross. And that face is turned away from Him. He is treated as a sinner, as the chief among sinners, for all the sins of the world are laid upon Him now. O sacred, suffering soul of Christ, who shall tell the anguish of its desolation upon Calvary! See Him as He drinks to the dregs this bitterest drop of His bitter chalice. Hear the cry of His breaking Heart: "My God, My God, why hast Thou forsaken Me!"

The lightest pain suffered by Him who was God as well as man, the least shedding of His most Precious Blood, was enough to redeem a thousand worlds. But He would pour it out to the last drop, that I might know how bad, how terrible a thing is sin.

Because I must be clothed with the best of everything—He must hang naked on the cross!

Because I am proud, and desire to be thought better than I am—He is treated as a sinner and a fool!

For my greediness, His tongue is tormented with vinegar and gall, His throat is parched with thirst!

Because I like to be comfortable in everything and hate the least little pain or inconvenience— His shoulders are furrowed with stripes, His hands and feet are bored with nails!

Because I can suffer nothing at all in satisfaction for my sins—He must be tortured from head to foot!

Because I have deserved to be abandoned by God—He is forsaken by His Father in His hour of direst need!

All this *for me!* Oh, if I had seen Him on Calvary, and known His pain was all for my sake, could I have found it in my heart to go away and sin against Him! Could I be as careless as I am? Was it worth His while to show me so much love, for the little bit of love I have given Him in return?

He need not have suffered all this. He was not obliged to bear all this for me. He might have left me to perish. But His Heart would not let Him. From the height of His cross He saw all the ages to come, all the men, women, and children that were to look to Him to save them from sin and hell. He saw me. He knew me just as I am. Did that sight comfort Him? Or did His eyes fill with tears as He thought how little I should care for Him after all, how little I mind wounding His Heart by my sins?

But He saw me preparing for confession now. He saw I should want now to be sorry for my sins. He was comforted by seeing me kneeling here to-day:

> To me the glazed eyes turn;
> For me the white lips part;
> Throbbing with love of me to its last pulse
> Is that dear Heart:

> And shall I leave His feet
>> Freely to sin again,
> Renewing with unpitying hand the cause
>> Of all His pain?
>
> Oh, let me hate all sin
>> For which my Saviour died,
> And love with all my strength this God of love,
>> Christ crucified!

Summer and winter a little bare-footed child was seen at the early Mass in the principal church of one of our big towns. Without book or beads, what could she be doing as she knelt there so still? Some one resolved to ask:

"Do you say your beads every morning at Mass?"

"Please, I haven't got no beads."

"Some other prayers then?"

"I don't know any Mass prayers."

"What are you doing all the time?"

"I looks up at big crucifix and I thinks—*as it was me that did it.*"

## God infinitely good in Himself

"God so loved the world as to give His only-begotten Son." (St. John 3.) And shall we not so love Him who has given us Jesus crucified, as to grieve with all our hearts for having offended Him!

From seeing how good God has been *to us*, we pass on easily to think how good He must be *in Himself*.

God has given me all that I have—my body, my soul, my health, my senses. Why am I not blind, or lame, or deformed like so many? He has given me my father and mother, my home, my friends, my education. How many children I see—children who have to save their souls as I have—yet who have fewer helps by far than God has given me—no one to love and care for them; to teach, and to warn them; to help them to get to heaven. What should I be now, were I in their place?

God watches over me as the most loving of fathers, providing plants, animals—all I need for food and clothing; books, games—all I need for my mind; the sacraments, Mass, Benediction, Holy Communion, holy inspirations and instructions—all I need for my soul. All the beauty I see in the sunshine and the flowers; all that delights me in scent or in song; all that makes me happy in the goodness and kindness of others, is God's gift to me, *to me*, as if He had no one else to think of. In everything He has made, He had me in view; for me He has been contriving and planning as though I were alone in the world. Oh, what a good, good God our God must be!

For notice this—If He can be so good to little weak creatures that can never be of any use to Him; if He wants to have them all round and about Him in a happy eternity, that He may delight in their joy—how good He must be *in Himself!* Is it hard to be sorry for having offended Him *because He is so good?* Is not perfect contrition the easiest as well as the best!

> Father, I love Thee, as a child should love
>     Whom Thou hast loved so well;
> Not for the joys prepared for me above,
>     Nor from the fear of hell:
> All that is Thine, Thy Heart, Thyself,
>     Freely Thou givest me;
> All that is mine, my heart, myself,
>     Freely I give to Thee!

Should any one of these thoughts about hell, heaven, the sufferings of our Lord, move you to sorrow for your sins, stay upon it. You need not go on to others, for you have found what you were seeking. Many considerations are offered, not that you may scamper through all, but that there may be a variety to suit different tastes and moods. It is because we hurry from one thought to another, that we are moved by none. The less we take to think about, the more fruit we often find. But—the rule applies here as everywhere—nothing is to be found without trouble. We must be willing to take pains. Look again at the bee. It does not simply alight on the flowers and wait for the sweet juice to come to it, but it thrusts its little sharp tongue down into the calyx and works vigorously till it gets what it wants.

Remember, then, when you want to rouse yourself to contrition, that it is not the number of motives you take, but the thoughtful pondering of one or two that will make you wish you had never had anything to do with sin, wish to tear yourself free of it, to hate its bad work in yourself or others.

You will have noticed that these motives for sorrow mount like the rungs of a ladder. All are useful and help us up to God. We should use all, but not all at once. The highest is perfect contrition. Ask God to put into your heart this best sorrow—sorrow for having offended Him *because He is so good*.

We perfect our contrition as we perfect our scales, by constant practice. Paderewski[1], proficient as he is, keeps his fingers in constant exercise. They were stiff once, because untrained, like our acts of contrition perhaps. And just as now they sweep the keys with perfect ease, so will acts of loving contrition, making sweet music in the ear of God, flow from our hearts when frequency has brought habit. We will make short acts of contrition, then, not only when preparing for confession, but at other times:

"My God, I do so wish I had never offended You."

"O God, I am sorry for everything, great or small, by which I have displeased You."

---

[1] Ignacy Jan Paderewski was a famous pianist and composer who also served as Prime Minister of Poland in 1919.

"Give me, my God, a loving sorrow for all my sins."

"My God, make me hate sin as You want me to hate it."

"My God, I am sorry for having offended You because You are so good."

"Jesus, my God, I love You above all things."

These acts are so short that we can put our whole heart into them. There is no time to get distracted. But though so short, the good they do is very great. They can be made everywhere and at any time—when we commit a fault, when we genuflect before the tabernacle, going up and down stairs, when we take holy water. But night—this is above all the time for them. "Sleep is death's younger brother, and so like him that I dare not trust him without my prayers." Always take care to make a good act of contrition after your examination of conscience at your night prayers, and again just before you get into bed. That act may be your last; you *may* wake before the judgment-seat of Christ. Be ready, and death need have no terrors for you.

Each act helps to form a habit, and a more blessed habit we could not have. Many and many a soul owes its salvation to the ease with which it turned to God by an act of contrition.

Two boys meet with a railway accident. One, when the shock comes, thinks only in a terror-stricken, stupefied way that he is going to die. He cries out, but his cry is not a prayer, and in the few minutes of time that remain to him he never thinks of God. Habits come out at death, and he has no such habit. The other is terror-stricken too—death is close at hand. But the very terror wakes up the habit of his life, and he cries: "My Jesus, mercy!"

We never know when death may overtake us. Our Lord bids us be watching always, for He will come like a thief in the night: "What I say to you, I say to all: Watch!" An act of contrition might save us if we had no time to make our confession. By the love then that you have for your soul, and to make its salvation sure, begin without delay to acquire the habit of making good acts of contrition.

◆

## IV. We must resolve by the grace of God to renounce our sins and to begin a new life for the future.

There can be no real sorrow for what we are going to take no pains to avoid. If you are really sorry for having spoilt your tennis-net by leaving it out at night, you will not leave the new one out. And if you are really sorry for having offended God by such and such a fault, you will take reasonable pains not to offend Him by repeating that fault.

Remember we have to make a *purpose* of amendment. Now a purpose is not a mere passing wish, it is a strong intention or determination, it is *the making up of our mind* about something. Clearly then it needs time and thought. This purpose, as has been said, is really part of our act of contrition, for there can be no true sorrow for the wrong we have done unless we intend not to do it again. Indeed, one of the ways of testing the reality of our contrition is to see if we are going to take any pains to do better for the time to come. The purpose of amendment we are bound to have is a firm determination to avoid all mortal sin and the proximate occasions of mortal sin. Let us see what these are.

When we have tripped on the pavement, or failed in an examination, we look back to find the cause. When we have fallen into sin we must look back to see what was the occasion. Any circumstance leading to sin is called an *occasion of sin*. It may be proximate or remote. A *proximate* occasion is one which usually leads us into sin. A *remote* occasion is one in which we sometimes though seldom commit sin. Persons, places, and things may all become occasions of sin, some to one person, some to another. Certain things, such as bad companions, improper conversations, bad books, are always proximate occasions of sin.

Each one of us is strictly bound to avoid what is a proximate occasion of mortal sin to him. Sometimes, by means of prayer, a more frequent use of the sacraments, and other precautions, a proximate occasion may be made remote. But should there be any person, place, or thing which, no matter what we do, always leads us into mortal sin, we are bound to keep away from it at any cost. Our Lord says, "If thy hand, or thy foot scandalize thee,"—that is, if something you care for as much as hand or foot, leads you to commit sin—"cut it off and cast it from thee. It is better for thee to go into life maimed or lame, than having two hands or two feet to be cast into everlasting fire." (Matt. 18.)

We should of course resolve to avoid venial sins too, and if we have these only to confess, we should pick out one at least, and make a firm resolve about that. If you cannot make up your mind what to choose, think what our Lord would advise, and you will make a good choice.

To be of any use, a resolution must be sensible. Here is one that is not sensible: "I am never going to commit a sin again. I am going to be bad in nothing and good in everything." The devil laughs at a resolution like that. But if instead of this I say—"I will avoid that dangerous occasion—I will say this aspiration when I am tempted—I will watch over myself at such a time, or when talking to such a person, so as to avoid *that fault*—I will try to lessen the number of times I fall; and when I do fall I will come back to God *at once* with an act of sorrow or love, and try again as if nothing had happened"—oh, the devil does not laugh at this. He cannot afford to laugh. For this means dead loss to him, the overthrow of all his plans. Any one keeping resolutions such as these, will come safely out of all his temptations and march over him up to a high place in heaven.

Remember lastly, we are to resolve *by the grace of God* to renounce our sins. We cannot do it of ourselves, by our own strength. But God has promised to help us always if we ask Him, and the weakest of us may say with David, "In the strength of my God, I shall go over a wall." (Ps. 17.) And with St. Paul, "I can do all things in Him who strengtheneth me." (Philipp. 4.)

It need hardly be said that if our sorrow and purpose of amendment are sincere, we shall be ready to do what is necessary to get our sins forgiven and to amend our life. To refuse to forgive one who has offended us, or to give back ill-gotten goods, or to restore as far as we can a good name when we have taken it away by calumny or detraction, would prove that we are not really sorry for our sins, and therefore not in fit dispositions to receive the Sacrament of Penance.

But now for a difficulty. If you are earnestly trying to serve God and to make good, fervent confessions, this thought is sure to strike you—"I go to confession often, I make good resolutions, and yet I am always falling into the same old faults. Does this show that I have not real contrition?"

Not necessarily. Our natural character lays us open to the same temptations, and the routine of our daily life brings round the same occasions. And therefore it is not surprising if we take the same faults to confession again and again. What we have to do is to lessen the number; to rid ourselves of them by degrees; to turn occasions of sin into occasions of victory; thus, as St. Augustine says, using them as steps by which to climb up to heaven.

We do not make a purpose of transfiguration—to become all at once entirely different from what we were—but a purpose of *amendment*. Mending is a gradual and a laborious process, whether it be the mending of a stocking or of a man-of-war. No one expects it to be done all at once. If God is patient with us, and willing to wait whilst we mend, why should we be so impatient with ourselves!

Just before going into the confessional, make another hearty act of sorrow for all the sins you are going to confess, and for some sin of your past life for which you are truly sorry. This confession of a past sin is a most excellent practice, if we remember it is done *for the sake of arousing contrition*. But nothing can be more useless—to say the least—than to confess it merely by routine. Hence it is well in our act of contrition to clearly include this sin.

In a few minutes you will be saying the *Confiteor*[1], that is, you will be confessing your sins before Almighty God and the grandees of the court of heaven. Think how ashamed you would be if you had to confess them before your father and mother, brothers, sisters, schoolfellows. Should you feel less shame to confess before God, the Holy of Holies; before Blessed Mary, conceived without sin; before angels and saints, standing without spot before the great white throne? The sense of shame does us good and helps us to sorrow. Think, too, that all that heavenly court looks down lovingly upon you, and is praying for you, and rejoices to see you purifying your soul in the Precious Blood to be ready for their company some day.

It happens, however, sometimes, that we have to wait, not a few minutes, but a long time at the confessional, and that having finished our preparation, we begin to look about and get distracted, going in at last tired and cross. This is a pity. If we like, we may say our beads then, or read "Starting afresh" (p. 74), or some of the Gospel stories at the end of the book. They will not distract us, but on the contrary, will help us to make a good act of contrition when our turn comes to go in.

---

1  This prayer of confession is still found in its original form in the Tridentine (or Extraordinary form) Mass, and in a slightly modified form in the Ordinary form, but is no longer used in the confessional, having been replaced with the Act of Contrition.

# IV
## Confession

Remember once more that you are going to confess your sins to our Blessed Saviour, who is waiting to hear you, to help you, to absolve you. Think of Him; tell it all to Him. This will take away any feeling of fear as to what the priest may think or say. Never hide anything in your conscience that makes it troubled or uncomfortable. If you have any difficulty in telling any sin, or do not know how to say it, begin with that sin, asking the priest to help you. Do not leave it to the end. The priest will never be angry with you. And as for a little pain or shame, we must willingly go through it to get the sin forgiven. Else we shall have the shame of hearing that sin told before the whole world at the Last Day. One prayer to our Lady for help, one brave effort, and you will be rewarded immediately by a flood of peace and happiness. Make each confession as if it were to be your last. Leave nothing to be said at some future time—when you feel better able to say it—when you come to die. Clear up everything now, so that whenever you leave the confessional you can say to yourself: "If this should be the last time I ever receive the sacrament, I think I could be content to meet our Lord at Judgment as I am now."

♦ *For an updated version of the form for confession, see p. 102* ♦

1. Kneeling down in the confessional, make the sign of the cross:

**In the name of the Father, and of the Son, and of the Holy Ghost. Amen.**

2. Ask a blessing:

**Pray, Father, give me your blessing for I have sinned.**

3. Say the first part of the *Confiteor*:

**I confess to Almighty God, to Blessed Mary ever a Virgin, to Blessed Michael the Archangel, to Blessed John the Baptist, to the holy Apostles, Peter and Paul, to all the Saints, and to you, Father, that I have sinned exceedingly, in thought, word, and deed, through my fault, through my fault, through my most grievous fault.**

**Since my last confession which was** (*so many weeks, or months ago,*) **I accuse myself of...**

**I also accuse myself of the sins of my past life, especially of...**

**For these and all my other sins which I cannot at present call to my remembrance, I am heartily sorry, purpose amendment for the future, and most humbly ask pardon of God and penance and absolution of you, my ghostly father.**

**Therefore I beseech the Blessed Mary ever a Virgin, Blessed Michael the Archangel, Blessed John the Baptist, the holy Apostles, Peter and Paul, all the Saints, and you, Father, to pray to the Lord our God for me. Amen.**

4. After confessing your sins, *leave them.* Do not begin to think if you have told all. Whatever you have forgotten is forgiven. Listen attentively to the advice of your confessor. Then, while he gives you absolution, renew your act of sorrow as if you were kneeling at the feet of Jesus and He Himself were absolving you.

If you have restitution to make, whether of good name or of anything else, and do not know how to do it, or if on any other point you want to know what you ought to do, ask your confessor's advice about it.

Returning to your place, thank God very heartily for the Precious Blood that has been applied to your soul and has cleansed it from all its stains. Say some psalm or hymn or prayer in thanksgiving.

> Hail, Jesus! hail, who for my sake
> Sweet Blood from Mary's veins didst take
>    And shed it all for me;
> Oh, blessed be my Saviour's Blood,
> My life, my light, my only good,
>    To all eternity.
>
> To endless ages let us praise
> The Precious Blood, whose price could raise
>    The world from wrath and sin;
> Whose streams our inward thirst appease,
> And heal the sinner's worst disease,
>    If he but bathe therein.
>
> O sweetest Blood, that can implore
> Pardon of God, and heaven restore,
>    The heaven which sin had lost:
> While Abel's blood for vengeance pleads
> What Jesus shed still intercedes
>    For those who wrong Him most.
>
> O to be sprinkled from the wells
> Of Christ's own Sacred Blood excels
>    Earth's best and highest bliss:
> The ministers of wrath divine
> Hurt not the happy hearts that shine
>    With those red drops of His!

> Ah! there is joy amid the saints
> And hell's despairing courage faints
>    When this sweet song we raise:
> Oh, louder then, and louder still,
> Earth with one mighty chorus fill,
>    The Precious Blood to praise!
>
> *Faber.* (100 DAYS' INDULGENCE.)

*or*

- Give praise to our God, all ye His servants; and you that fear Him, little and great. (Apoc. 19.)
- O give thanks to the Lord, because He is good: because His mercy endureth for ever and ever. (Daniel 3.)
- Let them say so that have been redeemed by the Lord, whom he hath redeemed from the hand of the enemy. (Ps. 106.)
- Bless the Lord, O my soul, and let all that is within me bless His holy Name. (Ps. 102.)
- Bless the Lord, O my soul, and never forget all that He hath done for thee. (Ps. 102.)
- What shall I render to the Lord, for all that He hath rendered to me? (Ps. 115.)
- O bless our God and make the voice of His praise to be heard. (Ps. 65.)
- I will cry to God, the most High, to God Who hath done good to me. (Ps. 56.)
- Bless the Lord, all ye servants of the Lord, who stand in the house of the Lord, in the courts of the house of our God. (Ps. 133.)
- O magnify the Lord with me, and let us extol His name together. (Ps. 33.)
- My soul doth magnify the Lord, and my spirit hath rejoiced in God, my Saviour. (Luke 1.)
- For He that is mighty hath done great things to me; and holy is His name. (Luke 1.)

- Blessed be the Lord, for He hath shown His wonderful mercy to me. (Ps. 30.)
- Blessed be the Lord for evermore. So be it, so be it. (Psalm 88.)

> Save me, my God, from sin!
> Let not its power enslave
> My feeble will, and ruthlessly destroy
> The soul thou diedst to save.
> By all Thy Blood outpoured,
> Mercy and grace to win,
> Forgive the past—and for the time to come,
> Save me, my God, from sin.

*or*

My God, I give you thanks with all my heart for forgiving me my sins once more. Oh, keep me from sin in the time to come! Give me grace to hate mortal sin more than death itself, and to avoid all occasions that would lead me into it. Once more I repent of all the sins of my past life. I renew my promises made in Baptism. I beg your blessing on my resolutions.

*or*

> O good Jesus, hear me,
> Within Thy wounds hide me,
> Never let me be separated from Thee,
> In the hour of my death call me
> And bid me come to Thee,
> That with thy saints I may praise Thee,
>     For all eternity.

You were told just now to leave your sins after confessing them; because anything forgotten was forgiven. Should anything grave have been forgotten and come to your mind later, you are not obliged to confess it before going to Holy Communion; mention it in your next confession.

Say your penance, if possible, before you leave the church. Say it humbly and gratefully. Though so short, it has more power of satisfaction than any other act of penance, because it acts sacramentally and has the merits of Christ's Precious Blood upon it. It therefore remits much of the punishment due to our sins, and *may* remit *all*, if our dispositions and state before God permit it.

Think of what your confessor told you to do or to avoid. Should you have any restitution to make, whether of good name or anything else, see how soon you can do it.

If you wish, you can make a visit to our Lady's altar to offer your resolutions to her and give them into her keeping. And do not forget to ask your good angel's help too. Those resolutions interest him very much indeed.

We were speaking long ago, at the beginning of these talks, of the devil's traps. He is a trapper by trade; all his work has to be done in that way, and of his snares there is no number.

But among them all, there are none more carefully set, none on which more hopes are built than those around the confessional. Why? Because if he can only frighten us away from the Sacrament of Penance, he need not trouble about anything else. We shall of course keep away from the altar-rails too, and then all is over with us; trials and temptations will be beyond our strength, and he may make sure of having us in his clutches in the end. "No confession, no Communion," he says to himself. And therefore he counts it a less gain to get us to commit sin, than to stay away from the sacrament he dreads.

He knows well what a store of precious grace is laid up for us there. He knows that we come away from it, not only with our sins forgiven, but with a title to receive as we need them, all actual graces for avoiding sin and doing good. Just as his soup or his coal-ticket gives the poor man a right to have food or firing as he requires it, so does the sacramental grace give a right to receive all actual graces to fulfil the end of the sacrament. It gives us light to see dangers and temptations, and strength to overcome them. It gives us self-knowledge and humility. It refreshes our souls continually with the blessed waters of contrition. It remits the temporal punishment due to our sins. It strengthens our will in good. It gives us courage in the work of overcoming our faults, particularly our predominant passion; and spirit—not only to rise promptly from our falls—but to turn those very falls to profit. And because it gives us joy in well-doing, it helps us to persevere with earnestness in the service of God. The measure in which we shall receive these graces will depend on the dispositions we bring to the sacrament. A large bucket will draw a large supply of water from the well, a smaller one will get less.

Our peace, our progress, our perseverance, depend so much on our making a fervent use of this sacrament, that we should try to improve our dispositions each time we approach it.

Remember these two things about every confession of your life:

1. *Never go in a hurry.* Do not put off the preparation to the last moment, but see that you have sufficient time to prepare.

2. *Never go into the confessional till your act of contrition is made.*[1] If you scramble over it, or make it a mere matter of routine, you will endanger the most important part of the sacrament and prepare for yourself great trouble of mind hereafter. Whatever else you forget when you come to our Lord's feet, whatever else you risk, be sure to secure one thing—your act of sorrow.

---

1 This is not to be confused with the prayer, which is said *in* the confessional. Mother Loyola is referring to the third of the four things necessary for a good confession: we must have contrition—that is, we must be truly sorry for the sins we are about to confess. See page 26 for more on this, including motives for sorrow.

Learn from your confessor how often you are to go to confession, and keep regularly to the appointed times.  If you foresee you will be prevented from going on the usual day, go before rather than after.  Never put it off if you can possibly help it.  The longer you defer, the more it will cost you to go.  You will lose your peace, your strength, your joy in the service of God.  Worst of all, you will accustom yourself to make light of the reproaches of conscience and to think little, first of small, then of great sins.  In this way has begun the loss of multitudes of souls.

# V
# Starting Afresh

And now we begin afresh. What is needed to succeed better than heretofore—to succeed, all things to the contrary notwithstanding—to succeed, so that one day we shall plant our flag on the walls of the Heavenly Jerusalem? We may sum it up in one word—"Pluck." Pluck to face bravely all the enemies we *must* face on our road. We know of three. But there is a fourth, more deadly, dangerous, and difficult to deal with than the other three put together. Its name is—*discouragement*. The world and our own bad inclinations are valuable allies of the devil, but he would part with both rather than with discouragement. It does more work for him among God's servants than sin itself can do. It fetters the strong sacraments. It makes effort feeble, and prayer cold, and generosity an unknown element in our dealings with God.

Like the master it serves, discouragement is thoroughly dishonest. It puts on the mask of humility and thus comes into the camp unsuspected, and gets a welcome instead of a rebuff. The chief weapons it uses against us are *our temptations* and *our falls*. We will notice its plan of operations, and take the falls first.

You have renewed once more that determination to keep your temper when So-and-so's exasperating ways threaten to rob you of it. But lo! at his very first word just now there was an explosion, and you are overthrown. At once discouragement is on the field: "Down again! the hundred and eleventh time this month. Not much use *your* trying, it seems. And now you are going to get up and go back to God, forsooth, as if nothing had happened! I wonder you have the face to do it. Anyhow, don't go back just yet. After treating Him so shabbily, it is hardly reverent, you know, to turn to Him quite directly with your act of sorrow. Wait awhile till you can mean it. Wait till your examination of conscience to-night. Besides, you are upset now and tired—you'll be better after a bit. There's no such violent hurry. Wait!"

Has discouragement ever said this to you?

Notice how many and different are the arguments brought to prevent you from turning at once to God with your act of sorrow: "*It is no use*—for you will never be any better. *It is bold and presumptuous*—for you do not deserve to be listened to this hundred and eleventh time. *It is irreverent*—for you have treated God shamefully and ought to be made to feel it. *And it is shamming*—for you are not really sorry, and probably there will be a hundred and twelfth fall before night."

The enemy uses his best logic to turn us to two things—downheartedness, and fear of returning to God at once. It is not so much our falls that he wants, as our dejection after them. For it is this that does us such harm. But "we are not ignorant of his devices," says St. Paul. (2 Cor. 2.) And we are more than a match for him, when, giving no ear to his wiles, we turn at once to our Heavenly Father Who with outstretched arms is calling us to Him:

"Come to Me, child, and I will put you right again. Never mind if it is the hundred and eleventh time. I will have patience with you and welcome you the thousand and eleventh time, if you will only come back to Me. You have treated Me shabbily—come and tell Me so. And whilst the words of sorrow are still on your lips, I will stop them with My kiss of forgiveness. You are afraid you will not mean them? But your very coming to Me so trustfully shows that you mean them. Do not be afraid of Me, child. Each time you come back after a fall, I feel for you more tenderly, I fold you closer to my Heart, I lay up for you another crown."

Had discouragement ever done a particle of good, men might be found to try it as they try drugs that lull pain for the moment, though they bring ruin later. But it does not help us even for an instant; it is a second misery added to the first. Whichever way we look at it, we find nothing to excuse it—not even a grievous sin. Nay, it is just then we can least afford discouragement. It is then we need all our trust in God. It was Peter's trust that saved him. It was Judas' mistrust that made him fall hopelessly away.

If even a grievous fall does not warrant discouragement, how much less do little daily slips? "For the just man shall fall seven times and rise again." (Prov. 24.) God expects these ups and downs in His service, and makes allowance for them: "Let not this thing discourage thee, for various is the event of war." (2 Kings 2.) "Fight like a good soldier, and if sometimes thou fall through frailty, rise up again with greater strength than before, confiding in My more abundant grace." (*Imit.* iii. 6.) Not less because you are undeserving, but more because of your need.

Remember how very easy our loving Lord has made forgiveness. One act of perfect contrition, with a wish for the Sacrament of Penance, and the guilt of even mortal sin is washed away. Any sacrament of the living or of the dead; any act of faith, or hope, or charity; any little act of mortification or kindness for God's sake; any sacramental, such as holy water, piously used—and the guilt, with much of the temporal pain of venial sin, is remitted, and the soul recovers its former beauty in the sight of God.

"The penance given us by the priest does not always make full satisfaction for our sins," the Catechism says, "we should therefore add to it other good works and penances and try to gain Indulgences." Those who are brave enough to act upon this advice sometimes impose on themselves a little penance when they break the resolution made at confession. Thus, for a burst of temper, an aspiration for the Holy Souls; for disobedience, a little act of self-denial at table; for a lie, a penny to the poor. They do not want to go to purgatory for their faults, and prefer to do a little easy penance here. You will say perhaps that they must always be mortifying themselves, and be always dull and dismal. Not at all. Such a practice makes one careful indeed, but so far from dull, that it is a capital recipe for keeping bright and joyous. Try it when you are down in the dismals, after a fall; you will prove its happy effects at once.

If, however, you have no mind to look out for penances, you will at least take in the spirit of penance, the little rubs and vexations of daily life, and say promptly when God sends you any cross, or trouble, or sickness, or pain, "Lord, Thy will be done, I take this for my sins!"

During the three years of our Lord's public life, the years of miracles, He was often working cures all day long. From morning till night, the blind, the deaf, the withered, the lame, the possessed were brought to Him, and "He, laying His hands on every one of them, healed them." Yet not always at once, not always at the first prayer. Sometimes He questioned, sometimes He cured by degrees, sometimes He even pretended to be unwilling to grant a cure earnestly asked. But never when the sick person was a leper. No questioning then, no delay;

not only no appearance of unwillingness, but those blessed hands and lips flew to their work. A leper knelt before Him: "Lord, if Thou wilt, Thou canst make me clean." "I will, be thou made clean." See the haste, the eagerness; the very words of the prayer caught up and turned into words of healing. Oh yes, He willed, He always willed, He willed most earnestly to cure the horrible disease which in His eyes was the figure of sin.

And if He made such haste to destroy the figure, will He delay to destroy sin itself? "O God, be merciful to me a sinner," cried the poor publican. "And he went down into his house justified," says our Lord. So it is still. Jesus is Saviour, and He loves to save. Quicker than a mother whose child has fallen and hurt itself, He runs at our first cry. And as she picks the little one up and rocks it in her arms with endearing words, and kisses the sore place to make it well, so does our loving Lord take us up, and soothe us, and fold us to His Heart, thinking more in His tender pity of the hurt we have done ourselves than of the injury we have done to Him.

A wrong view of our faults leads straight to discouragement, sometimes to despair. The same may be said of our temptations. There are people, who in spite of all they have heard or read, persist in acting as if temptation and sin were one and the same thing. A thought comes into their mind, and instantly they are overwhelmed with trouble and dismay. They forget that the thoughts of the bad angels are no more ours than the thoughts of the good angels, and that, as St. Ignatius reminds us, we shall no more be punished for the one than we shall be rewarded for the other. They forget that unless by our free-will and consent we make our own the suggestions of the evil one, there can be no sin. A thought may refuse to go out of our mind, or after it has been sent out, may come again and again, teasing and tiring us. And this without the smallest sin on our part. Not only without sin, but with great merit. It actually gives us a claim to reward, for as long as our will says "No," we are fighting God's battle and meriting a higher place in heaven. A good way to keep our souls in peace and to conquer the enemy effectually, is to form a habit of turning to God at once by some short, fervent prayer: "My God, I love Thee!" "Lord, Thou knowest that I love Thee!"

Of course, we must not run into temptation of our own accord, for he that loveth danger shall perish in it. (Ecclus. 3.) But when without our seeking it comes in our way, God will take care of us. By avoiding unsafe companions and dangerous reading, by going often to confession and Communion, by praying in time of temptation, and remembering that God Who loves us is present and sees all, we shall be kept safe.

Let us take a lesson from our Army in the South African Campaign of 1899 and 1900.[1] Did the Generals yield to despondency and surrender because they were sorely pressed; because the enemy cut off communication, and shot down our officers, and shelled our armoured trains? Because, day after day, they had to fight a concealed enemy, to be on the alert always, prepared for attack in the most unlikely places?

"For God's sake, men of the King's Royal Rifles, make a stand," shouted the Major in command, when his regiment faltered for a moment at Spion Kop before the tremendous fire.[2] "Charge!" And with a cheer he rallied them, and stopped the advance of the enemy.

Was there any wavering among the women and children

---

1   The Second Boer War, fought between the British and the Boers—descendants of the original Dutch settlers of South Africa. Of all the British conflicts fought between 1815 and the 1914, it was the bloodiest, longest and most expensive, and involved a great deal of guerilla fighting.

2   The Battle of Spion Kop (or *Spy Hill*) was fought in January 1900 as part of the campaign to relieve the siege of the town of Ladysmith, South Africa, 21 miles to the northwest. It was a fierce battle as the British attempted to hold the hilltop under heavy artillery fire.

huddled together in the bombproof shelters of Mafeking?[1] Was there a word about surrender, as month after month the weary siege dragged on, and starvation stared them in the face? We should have expected, at least, that the gallant little town would have presented a dreary aspect all that time. Not a bit of it. When they might venture above ground, and move to and fro about their wrecked and ruined homes, the people made the best of the situation. There were the siege games of the children, who played at bombardments in cunningly-devised trenches. There were shows, concerts, tournaments, bazaars, kept going continually, for the wise Colonel knew the necessity of cheerfulness if the place was to hold out. "It has been the merriest siege in history," we were told. Yet it was certainly one of the closest and bitterest, and to all appearance, one of the most hopeless. But the spirit of leader and officers, of old and young, rose with the need, and up to the moment of relief they bore bravely pain, and hardship, and weariness, and suspense, looking trustfully for the help which they knew *must* come.

Dec. 12, 1899, Baden-Powell wrote to his mother: "This is our 60th day of the siege," (there were 158 to come), "and I do believe we're beginning to get a little tired of it, but I suppose like other things it will come to an end some day. I have got such an interesting collection of mementoes of it to bring home."

So may we all have, if we behave ourselves manfully and show a soldierly spirit. Let us make ours a merry siege as far as we can. When relief came at last to Ladysmith and Mafeking, the children were found worthy of special honour for the pluck they had shown under trial.

---

1 Mafeking, a town in the North-West Province of South Africa, near the border with Botswana, was besieged at the beginning of the Second Boer War. The siege lasted 217 days, and made Colonel Robert Baden-Powell a national hero.

Compare *our* situation with that of our brave troops, and see if we have anything to warrant discouragement. All that they had to keep up their hearts we have—a skilled leader, examples of valour before our eyes, the assurance of succour if we will only hold out. Have we any of the grounds for despair which might well have overthrown them? None. We know we shall never be tried beyond our strength. We know that even our deepest wounds need never prove fatal. We know that no one can cut off our communication; that every need is known at Home; that superabundant help is at hand always. Where, then, is there any excuse for the poor-spirited vice that eats away all our strength? Our temptations certainly do not warrant it! Do our falls? Why, we can turn them all into occasions of merit by humbling ourselves readily, rising instantly, returning to God trustfully. Fancy what a stir there would have been at Ladysmith, or Mafeking, if—by some marvellous discovery doing honour to the close of the century—defeat could have been made to pave the way to victory; all losses been repaired; the wounded healed; the dead restored to the ranks. This can be an every-day occurrence with us—and *we are discouraged!*

Whenever during the autumn of 1899 a shop in London or in the provincial towns exhibited a map of South Africa, a crowd of people could be found at any time of the day gazing at it with eager interest, especially when the positions of the troops were marked by flags.

But what was the general concern compared with the intense anxiety of those who had friends at the front—a father, a son, a brother, within range of the enemy's fire! How the War Office was besieged by them; how the lists of killed and wounded were scanned by straining eyes and trembling hearts!

So are our movements followed with keenest interest by the Home-Country above. Not one there but has friends at the front. Oh, how intently we are watched; with what fellow-feeling, what alternations of hope and fear! Every hour of stout resistance, every repulse of the enemy, every return to the charge after defeat, is hailed with acclamation by the great multitude that no man can number, standing before the throne and in sight of the Lamb. Would not this be encouragement enough, reward enough! But there is more than this. More—a thousand times more to us than the plaudits of angels and saints—is a word sounding in our hearts and thrilling them through and through—a word which makes us feel that to fight for Him is happiness even here—the word of the Leader saying to us: "Well done, good and faithful servant. (Matt. 25.) Be thou faithful unto death and I will give thee the crown of life." (Apoc. 2.)

Stories to read whilst I am waiting my turn

## The Pool of Bethsaida

Had you lived in Jerusalem, nineteen hundred years ago, you might every day have seen a very sad, and, at times, a very wonderful sight. There was in the Holy City a pond called the Pool of Bethsaida. It had five porches, covered over to keep out sun and rain. These porches were always filled with sick people—blind, deaf, lame, ill in all kinds of ways. They were lying about on every side. You will wonder why they were not at home in bed. What were they doing by the pond? They were watching the water. For this Pool of Bethsaida was not a common pond. Something very wonderful happened there. At certain times an angel came down from heaven and moved the water, and the first sick person who went in after it had been moved was cured of his sickness. No one knew when the angel would come, so the poor people were there always. Day after day they lay there, watching with sad eyes the water that stretched still as glass before them.

All at once it began to move, as if a breeze had stirred it. Oh, the change in that dull place then! The eager cries on every side, the outstretched hands, the call for help, the fierce striving and struggling of those nearest the water to get in first! A hush—

and then a cry of joy that filled the place, as one, all dripping, came bounding back, over beds and benches and crutches, and sick still creeping to the water's edge—came with life and health in every limb, walking, and leaping, and praising God! One only. The rest, sad and disappointed, went back to their old places to watch and wait again. Poor sick people, how tired they were! Some of them had been waiting for years, some almost all their lives.

If you go into a Catholic church on a Saturday evening you will see a number of people round the confessional. Their souls are sick, and they are waiting to go into that little place to be restored to health. No sad faces need be seen among them, for that place is not like the Pool of Bethsaida, where only one was cured. Every one who has tried to get ready, will be healed when his turn comes. No matter how sick he is, how many sins are on his soul, or how bad they are—he will be healed. And if he gets sick again and comes again as he ought, he will be healed again. As often as he comes He will be healed. Oh, how grateful we ought to be to our Blessed Lord for making His Pool in the Catholic Church so much happier a place than the one at Jerusalem long ago! Think of this when you are waiting for your turn to go in. And if sometimes you are tired of waiting, think of the poor people at Jerusalem lying for years by the Pool of Bethsaida, and thank Him that you have not to wait like them. You can thank Him too when you see the people come out of the confessional cured. You can join their good angels who are like their servants, and have helped them to get ready to go down into that blessed Pool, the Precious Blood of Jesus, where all their sickness has been taken away.

## The Ten Lepers

One day when our Lord was going to Jerusalem, a great crowd with Him as usual, He was met by ten men who were lepers. They were a horrible sight; faces and limbs eaten away by the dreadful disease; covered with sores that no kind hand ever dressed. For leprosy brought with it all manner of miseries—disgrace, banishment from home, the loss of all they had, of all they loved. This was the leper's lot. Instead of being helped and cared for in their pitiable state, they were forsaken even by their nearest and dearest. They might not live among other men, nor touch what other men touched, nor drink of the wells where other men drank. Driven out of towns, they wandered about in the wilds among brute beasts. There the chance passer-by would hear their doleful warning cry: "Unclean! Unclean!"

These ten poor men had heard that our Lord was a great wonder-worker, and that He was very kind, and healed the sick, and they thought He would perhaps have pity on them. So when they saw Him a long way off, they began to cry out to Him, "Jesus, Master, have mercy on us." At once His tender Heart was filled with pity, and He called them to Him. "Go, show yourselves to the priests," He said. And as they went, they were healed. No more pain or disgrace, no more dismal, lonely life apart from their fellow-men. They were free to go home and be happy once more, with all they loved about them. Oh, what a joyful change for these poor men!

Now what do you suppose was their first thought when they found themselves cured? Surely to run back to Jesus and thank Him again and again for His goodness to them. Would you believe it? One, only one went back. The others never so much as troubled themselves to return and say, "Thank you." Our Lord felt this ingratitude keenly. When this man fell down on his face before Him, giving thanks, He said sadly to those about Him: "Were there not ten made clean, and where are the nine? There is no one found to return and give thanks to God but this stranger."

We will not make Him sad like this. We will never be ungrateful after confession. We will go back to our places and thank Him with all our heart for taking away the leprosy of sin, and making our souls pure and beautiful in His sight, fit to be the companions in our Heavenly Home, of Himself and His Blessed Mother and the holy angels.

## The Prodigal Son

Two boys had a happy home. Their father loved them so dearly that he shared with them all he had. He thought nothing too good for them, nothing too much to spend upon them, He liked to see them enjoy themselves, and was always planning for them some little treat or pleasant surprise. They lived in his companionship always, loving and loved, trusting him perfectly, wishing for no pleasures but such as he provided for them, such as could be shared with him.

But after awhile a change came over the younger son. He grew restless and discontented; wanted to have everything his own way; wanted other enjoyments than those his father could give or approve. He grumbled at the wise rules of his father's house. Why need there be any rules? Why was any one set over him? It was very hard to have to do what he was told from morning till night. At last he made up his mind to leave home and go far away to some place where he could be his own master and do as he liked.

In vain did his father warn him of the misery he was going to bring on himself, and entreat him to stay where he was, with him in his happy home. The boy would listen to nothing. His mind was made up. He would go where he could have his own way, where there would be no one to check or advise him.

One day, the good father told his boys that when he was dead all his things would be divided between them, and each should have half. The elder one looked sad when he heard this. But the younger said to himself: "I will have my share now; then I shall be able to get away from home." So when his father was alone, he went to him and said, "Father, give me the money now that I am to have when you are dead." His father looked at him, not angrily, but sadly. If he had a favourite, it was this, his younger child. He looked at him, and there were tears in his eyes. But he said nothing, and went away and divided all his goods, and gave him what he asked. The boy put together as many things as he could carry, and very early next morning, before any one was about, he left home.

It was spring-time, and trees and hedgerows were beautiful in their robe of tender green. The birds sang gaily above his head, as with a light step he went whistling down the hill. He stopped for a few minutes beside the well to get a drink, and to count his money. Then on he went again till the white road turned, and he was out of sight. Yes, out of sight. The eyes dimmed with tears that were watching him from the high window, could see him no longer.

Through the lanes, and across the meadows, by the river, past villages, where the children were playing in the doorways, over lonely moors, he wandered on, stopping to look at anything that amused him, eating when he was hungry, resting when he was tired—he could do as he liked now. So the first day went, and the next, and the next. Many days, till he came into a strange country. It was far away from home. His father would never find him here, or get any news of him. "I will stay in this place," he said, "and enjoy myself. I shall do as I like all day long, then I shall be happy." Was he? Let us see.

For a time amusements and pleasures took up all his thoughts and made him forget his home and all he had left behind. But after awhile he began to tire of these things, and then his heart felt empty and lonely, and a great sadness came over him.

Having no good father to watch over him and help him to choose his friends, he began to go with bad companions, who soon made him as bad as themselves. They did not really care for him, and liked him only because he gave them treats. His money went very fast, and he had soon spent it all. His clothes were worn out, and he could not buy new ones. He expected his friends would help him now. But when they saw his money was finished, they all left him. At this time there came a great famine in the land, and he saw that He must either work for his living or starve. He went and hired himself to a man who sent him into the country to feed his swine. It was dirty work, and he got very little for it. He was so hungry that he would gladly have eaten the husks that were given to the swine. But not so much as this was bestowed upon him. In his misery he thought of the old times in his father's house before he began to be disobedient and discontented, the happy days when he sat at his father's table, and sported about under his father's eye. He longed to bring back those days. He remembered how kind his father had always been to him, how well off he had been at home. Why, even the servants there had plenty to eat, whilst he was here dying of hunger!

A thought struck him. "I will arise and go to my father, and say to him: Father, I have sinned against heaven and before thee, I am not now worthy to be called thy son: make me as one of thy hired servants."

It was a good thought; he could not have had a better. But other thoughts came too. Would his father have him back, an ungrateful, undutiful son, who had turned his back on home and wasted all his money? Again, what would people say? What if he were to meet on the road those who had known him when he was almost a spoilt child, well-dressed and cared for, the honoured son of a noble house? These doubts flashed through his mind. But he did not heed them. He did not delay one moment. Rising at once, he gathered his tattered clothes around him and set off on his way home.

Now his father had not forgotten him all this time. He was very unhappy when his son went away, and his heart was fretting after him still. "Oh, if he would come back," he often said. Morning and night his lost child was in his mind, and many a time he went to a high window and looked out over the white, dusty road, hoping to see something of him.

And so it happened that just as the poor boy came in sight of his home, his father saw him. He was a great way off, and not a bit like the lad who had gone off in such spirits long ago. Scarcely covered by his rags, without shoes on his feet, he looked what he was—a beggar. No one who passed him on the road knew him. But his father knew him, and tears trickled down the old man's cheeks as he watched his prodigal child coming nearer and nearer, and saw how pale and thin and ill he looked. He came on slowly, for the sharp stones were cutting his feet; he was hungry, and oh! so tired. His father could bear the sight no longer. He came quickly downstairs and set off running on the road to meet him, thinking of all the kind things he would say. But when he came up to him, he could not speak a word; he could only throw his arms round his neck and kiss him, while happy tears ran down his face.

"Father," the poor boy began, "I have sinned against heaven and before thee. I am not worthy to be called thy son. Make me,"—he was going on to say—but his father did not hear him. He was so glad to have him back that he did not listen to anything. He was calling out to the servants who had run after him to see what was the matter: "Bring quickly the best robe and put it on him, and put shoes on his feet. Be quick, be quick, that no one may see him like this and think he is in disgrace. And kill the fatted calf and get a feast ready. And let us be merry and happy, because this my son was dead and is come to life again, he was lost and is found."

Is not this a beautiful story? And the best thing about it is, that it is our Lord's story. He told it to show us how good and kind our Heavenly Father is, and that we must never be afraid to go back to Him if we have gone away by sin. No matter how bad the sin was, we must not be afraid.

When we break His commandments to please ourselves, we are satisfied perhaps, for a little while. But it is only for a little while. Then we begin to be unhappy. We wish we had not gone away from our Father; we should like to go back to Him. But we think He is angry with us and does not want to be friends with us again. He knows we feel like this. So He tries to comfort us and coax us back to Himself. "Come back to Me, and be My child as you were before," He says when one of His children goes away from Him. And when the child comes back by a good confession, and strikes his breast and says: "Father, I have sinned, through my fault, through my fault, through my most grievous fault," He is so glad to see him again that He quite forgets how bad he has been. He calls to His priests: "Be quick and bring the first robe—the beautiful robe of grace I gave him in Baptism, and put it on him again. And let all the angels and saints be glad and rejoice because My son was dead and is come to life again; he was lost and is found."

## St. Mary Magdalen

One day a rich man named Simon asked our Blessed Lord to dine at his house. Jesus went and sat down to dinner with a great many people, the rich man's friends, who had been invited. Some one else went, some one who was not invited and who was no friend of the rich man. A woman named Mary Magdalen wanted our Blessed Lord, and hearing He was to be at Simon's house, she determined to go to Him there. She had done many bad things, but she was sorry for them and wanted to be forgiven. She knew many people went to our Lord to be cured when their bodies were sick, and she thought He would perhaps cure her poor sick soul. Simon would not like to see her in the room where he was having his feast, and all his friends would look crossly at her. But she did not mind. If Jesus would say He forgave her, she did not care what others said. But would He forgive her? He was very holy. He could not bear sin. Would He be angry with her? Mary Magdalen did not know. But she had seen His face. It was so kind that she thought He must be kind too, and would not drive her from Him.

So she went to the house with a box of sweet-smelling oil, the best thing she had at home. She wanted to give it to Jesus to show Him how sorry she was for her sins. When she got into the room where the people were at dinner, every one looked at her. They lifted up their eyes and their hands and spoke low down to each other, and said how shocked they were to see Mary Magdalen in the same room with them. But she did not mind. She raised her eyes once to see where Jesus was, and then she went to Him straight and knelt down at His feet.

In those days people did not sit at table as we do now. They lay on sofas. So it was easy for Mary Magdalen to go and kneel down at our Lord's feet. She looked at Him to see if He was going to send her away. And as she looked at His beautiful face, so grave and yet so sweet, she thought of her sins; and tears ran down her cheeks on to His feet. She wiped them away with her long hair and stooped down and kissed His feet. Kissed them many times, and then the tears ran down again. She had not known Him long, but she loved Him dearly, and was bitterly sorry she had ever displeased Him and made Him sad. Again and again she wiped the tears away. And then she took her box of ointment and poured her sweet-smelling oil upon His feet.

Now the master of the house was watching all this time. He looked first at Mary Magdalen, and then at our Lord. At last he said to himself: "If Jesus of Nazareth were a holy man as people say, He would know this woman is a sinner, and He would be angry with her and drive her away from Him." Simon did not speak, but our Lord saw the thought in his mind, and turning to him, He said:

"Simon, I have something to say to thee."

"Master, say it."

"There was a man who had two debtors. One owed him a very large sum, the other not so much. But neither of them could pay him, and he forgave them both. Which of the two loved him best?"

"I suppose the one to whom he forgave most."

"You have judged right. Now look at this woman. You think

her a great sinner. See if she is not better than you. You gave Me no water for My feet, but she has washed them with her tears and with her hair has wiped them. You gave Me no kiss, but she since she came in has not ceased to kiss My feet. You did not anoint My head. But she has poured her sweet ointment on My feet. Therefore I say to you, many sins are forgiven her because she has loved much."

Then He turned to the woman and said: "Thy sins are forgiven thee; go in peace."

Happy Mary Magdalen, to hear those words from the lips of Jesus! We shall not hear them from His lips when we go to confession. But the words of absolution we shall hear—what more do we want? Our Lord forgives in heaven what His priest forgives on earth, for He has said, "Whose sins you shall forgive they are forgiven." And so He really says to us after confession as to blessed Mary Magdalen, "Thy sins are forgiven thee, go in peace."

# The Good Thief

Our Blessed Lord's gentleness to sinners was so well known that His enemies reproached Him with it. "The Friend of sinners," they called Him. And He loved the name. He loved to have sinners about Him during His life, and He was not ashamed to have them for His companions in death. Two poor men were brought out of prison to die with Him on Calvary. They had led bad lives, and now were going to death and to judgment with unrepenting hearts. The Heart of Jesus ached for them. He thought more of them than of Himself.

They were to be His companions in disgrace for a few short hours: He wanted them to be His companions forever in glory. And so when the procession to Calvary was forming, and they were brought near to where He stood, the cross on His shoulder, He turned to them with love in His eyes. But they had come out of their prison raging against Him. "But for Him," they said, "we should not have had to die to-day." They met His look with a scowl of fierce hate, and when again and again on the way a halt was called, and they heard He had fallen to the ground, there was no pity for Him in their hearts.

The shouts and cries that followed our Lord up the steep of Calvary, stopped when the crowd came to the place where He was to be crucified. The crosses were thrown on the ground; the soldiers cleared a space around them; and there was silence, broken only by the sound of the hammer, whilst the dreadful work of crucifixion went on, only that Jesus said again and again as they drove in the nails: "Father, forgive them, for they know not what they do!" But when He was raised aloft in the sight of all, a hoarse shout went up to Him; and presently, like the swelling tide, a sea of angry faces swept onward, wave after wave, towards the spot where the cross was reared. There it stopped, but only to turn all its fury against Him Who hung there trembling with agony in every limb.

"Vah, Thou that destroyest the temple of God and in three days dost rebuild it; save Thy own self: if Thou be the Son of God, come down from the cross."

"He saved others; Himself He cannot save." (St. Matt. 27.)

The word "saved" roused afresh the rage of the thieves on either side, and they cried to Him in mocking tones: "If Thou be Christ, save Thyself and us." (St. Luke 23.)

Suddenly, in the midst of his blasphemy, the thief on the right stopped short. His eyes had lighted on the face that, white in the gathering darkness, was turned towards heaven. It was shameful in its disfigurement—bleeding, swollen, discoloured with bruises. No beauty there to draw. Yet, somehow, it drew him strangely. Our Lord had promised that when He should be lifted up, He would draw all hearts to Himself. The first to feel the effects of this promise were His two companions in death, the thieves on His right and left. He drew them both. Both were being redeemed by Him, to both he offered the Precious Blood that from hands, and feet, and head—from a thousand wounds was trickling to the ground. To both He gave the grace to see in Him—not a tortured criminal, but the long expected Messiah, the King of Israel, foretold by the prophets. Both were drawn. But they were not obliged to come by repentance to Him who drew them. The promise was to *draw*, not to force. God's way is to offer us grace and then to wait and see what we do. If we take what He gives, He gives more. But we can refuse. We can open our hearts when grace comes, or we can close them and shut it out.

The thief to the left shut his heart against the grace that came to it from the Heart of Jesus. "Save Thyself and us!" Unless that prayer was answered in the way he wanted it to be answered, he would have none of the faith, hope, love, sorrow that were knocking at his door. Jesus wanted to save him. He was hanging there on purpose to save him. He was ready to free him for eternity from all sorrow and pain, if only his heart would let itself be softened. No: the poor wretched man, who was fast losing all he held dear in this life, would lose everything he might hope for in the next, rather than humble himself to say he was sorry for the sins of his life.

Oh, what a terrible power we have of hardening our hearts! Midnight darkness had covered the world at noon; the crosses were rocking to and fro with the shock of the earthquake; the rough Roman centurion was striking his breast and saying, "Indeed, this was the Son of God!" and still the thief on the left said, "*No*" to the voice of God within him, calling on him to turn to Jesus, and have his sins forgiven while there was yet time. He turned his face the other way that he might not see those pleading eyes. He shut his ears when the words of absolution went from the cross to his companion. He hardened his heart more and more as the long hours dragged on, and his pain became each moment more and more intolerable. And so in his rage and despair, with his Saviour by his side, and with the Precious Blood shed for him all around—he breathed his last.

And what about his companion? Strangely but strongly his heart was being drawn to Him who hung so still beside him. "Let Christ the King of Israel come down from the cross and we will believe in Him," the Jews had cried, in mockery, nay, he himself had cried out mockingly awhile ago. But now all was changed. And as he looked upon the upturned face, so calm in its awful agony, he felt, he knew that this was indeed a King. Christ the King of Israel had not come down from the cross, yet he believed in Him. He turned to Jesus:

"Lord, remember me, when Thou shalt come into Thy Kingdom." It was all he said. No prayer, only that cry for a remembrance. But there was faith, and hope, and charity, and sorrow for the sins of a life in those three words: "Lord, remember me." And Jesus said:

"Amen, I say to thee, this day thou shalt be with Me in Paradise."

What did that poor thief feel then! He, but just now a criminal in the sight of God and men, dying a terrible death, and deserving punishment more terrible still after death—to hear such words as these!

Truly Christ our Lord was a King, and gave like a King with royal hand, not simply what was asked, not a remembrance only, but what the poor thief could never have asked—forgiveness of all sin and remission of punishment; final perseverance and a happy death; and paradise in his Master's company before the sun should set. All this in answer to three words: "Lord, remember me!" Is our Lord hard to appease? Is it hard to get forgiven?

After his absolution how different everything looked to the good thief! The pain of the cross had still to be borne, and a cruel death by the breaking of his legs. But he feared none of these things as he hung there peaceful and patient by his Master's side, his eyes fixed on his Master's face. He heard the last loud cry. He saw the head droop on the breast. He saw the Sacred Heart opened by the lance. For a little while he hung there; lonely now, and in bitter pain, but trusting himself to Jesus, and glad to suffer in penance for his sins. And then the end came.

Our Lord was in Limbo, turning the place of waiting into heaven for the holy prisoners there. Adam and Eve, Abraham, Isaac, Moses, David were gathered round Him, adoring, praising, rejoicing—when there was a hush—a new arrival. One entered, the first saint of the New Law, and quick as light, sped through the throng to his Master's side—it was the soul of the poor thief!

Have we not a good Master! Must He not be good, infinitely good, to forgive the sins of a life—because of one act of sorrow and trust!

### Updated form for Confession.

1. Kneeling down in the confessional make the sign of the Cross:

**In the name of the Father, and of the Son, and of the Holy Ghost.**

2. Ask a blessing:

**Bless me, Father, for I have sinned.**

3. Say how long it has been since your last confession:

**It has been ___weeks since my last confession.**

4. Tell your sins in the way you can remember them best. Say how often or about how often you have done them. If you are nervous or afraid, ask the Priest to help you. At the end say:

**For these sins and all the sins of my past life, I am truly and heartily sorry, especially for the sin of (say which sin).**

5. After confessing your sins, *leave them.* Do not begin to think if you have told all. Whatever you have forgotten is forgiven. Listen attentively to the advice of your confessor. Then, while he gives you absolution, renew your act of sorrow

as if you were kneeling at the feet of Jesus and He Himself were absolving you.

If you have restitution to make, whether of good name or of anything else, and do not know how to do it, or if on any other point you want to know what you ought to do, ask your confessor's advice about it.

Now recite the Act of Contrition:

**O my God, I am heartily sorry for having offended Thee, and I detest all my sins because I dread the loss of heaven and the pains of hell, but most of all, because they have offended Thee, my God, who are all good and deserving of all my love. I firmly resolve, with the help of Thy grace, to confess my sins, to do penance, and to amend my life. Amen.**

6. When the priest says the words of absolution:

"I absolve thee from thy sins, in the name of the Father, and of the Son, and of the Holy Ghost," bow down your head, make the sign of the Cross and say:

**Amen.**

7. The priest will dismiss you, saying "Go in peace, your sins are forgiven." Say:

**Thank you, Father.**

8. Come out of the confessional, and go to your place with your eyes cast down. Say your penance right away.

Thank God very heartily for the Precious Blood that has been applied to your soul and has cleansed it from all its stains. Say some psalm or hymn or prayer in thanksgiving. (*see page 68*)

Additional titles available from

# St. Augustine Academy Press

Books for the Traditional Catholic

### Titles by Mother Mary Loyola:

Blessed are they that Mourn
Confession and Communion
Coram Sanctissimo (Before the Most Holy)
First Communion
First Confession
Forgive us our Trespasses
Hail! Full of Grace
Heavenwards
Holy Mass/How to Help the Sick and Dying
Home for Good
Jesus of Nazareth: The Story of His Life Written for Children
The Child of God: What comes of our Baptism
The Children's Charter
The Little Children's Prayer Book
The Soldier of Christ: Talks before Confirmation
Welcome! Holy Communion Before and After

### Tales of the Saints:

A Child's Book of Saints by William Canton
A Child's Book of Warriors by William Canton
Illustrated Life of the Blessed Virgin by Rev. B. Rohner, O.S.B.
Legends & Stories of Italy by Amy Steedman
Mary, Help of Christians by Rev. Bonaventure Hammer
The Book of Saints and Heroes by Lenora Lang
Saint Patrick: Apostle of Ireland
The Story of St. Elizabeth of Hungary by William Canton

Check our Website for more:

# www.staugustineacademypress.com

www.ingramcontent.com/pod-product-compliance
Lightning Source LLC
Chambersburg PA
CBHW030000050426
42451CB00006B/75